WORCESTERSHIRE'S
HISTORIC
PUBS

WORCESTERSHIRE'S
HISTORIC
PUBS

KEITH TURNER & JAN DOBRZYNSKI

SUTTON PUBLISHING

Sutton Publishing, an imprint of
NPI Media Group Limited
Cirencester Road · Chalford · Stroud
Gloucestershire · GL6 8PE

First published 2007

Title page photograph: The sign of the
Brewers Arms, West Malvern. Almost all
country pubs from the nineteenth century
or earlier produced their own beer
(or cider).

British Library Cataloguing in Publication Data
A catalogue record for this book is available from the
British Library.

ISBN 978-0-7509-4421-2

Typeset in 10.5/14pt Photina.
Typesetting and origination by
NPI Media Group Limited.
Printed and bound in England.

The Whitty Pear women's Morris dancers peforming at the Mug House, Claines – one of many
pubs in the county where the Morris tradition is maintained.

CONTENTS

The Black Boy, Bewdley. A typical example of a half-timbered pub in which Worcestershire, urban as well as rural, abounds.

The epitome of a Worcestershire historic pub: the Fleece Inn at Bretforton.

PREFACE

With well over 500 establishments to choose from in this quintessentially English county, with its centuries-old traditions of hop growing, cider making and brewing, selecting 60 of Worcestershire's historic pubs for special mention was never going to be an easy task – but it was one we applied ourselves to assiduously! In fact, we found more than enough to fill this book, so have tried to pick a fair representation of the county's treasures with regard to their age, type and geographical location. North or south, east or west, town or country – they are not *the* best 60 pubs in Worcestershire, for that is an impossible judgement to make, but they are certainly 60 *of* the best.

Included here are prime examples of riverside pubs – the famous Severn 'mug houses' – wayside inns, canal and railway pubs, and home-brew pubs, as well as the mainstay of every community, the local. Large or small, plain or plush, town or hamlet, half-timbered, stone or brick, each establishment is unique in its own very special way.

All have been visited and revisited, and are fully recommended to anyone in search of good beer, cider, food, a great atmosphere, a slice of Worcestershire history – and the odd quirk, curiosity, witch and ghost or two.

K. Turner & J. Dobrzynski, Kidderminster, 2007

Dark doings in the Fir Tree Inn, Dunhampstead.

The Bell & Cross at Holy Cross, Clent, with its distinctive signs lit by the midday sun. As will be seen, the adoption of religious images for pub names was a common practice.

INTRODUCTION

There is nothing which has yet been contrived by man, by which so
much happiness is produced as by a good tavern or inn.
Samuel Johnson, in James Boswell's *Life of Samuel Johnson*, 1791

Every pub has a history, and the pubs of Worcestshire are no exception to this rule. Old or modern, they all carry with them in their location, layout, architectural features and even size, clues as to when they were built, and why. Some, of course, carry more clues than others, for a great many of them have been remodelled extensively – or even demolished and replaced by a totally new building which then begins to accumulate a new history all of its own. . .

The Eagle & Spur, by the crossroads in Cookley. Pubs were commonly sited where several roads or streets met in order to catch as many passers-by as possible. It was also a logical location for a village or town clock – as in this case, installed in 2000 to commemorate the millennium.

Good landlords take great pride in the appearance of their pubs. Here, a great deal of time and effort has gone into making the front door of the Mug House at Bewdley look delightfully enticing.

Broadly speaking, the oldest pubs in Worcestershire, like those elsewhere in Britain, began life in one of three ways: as largely unregulated ale or cider houses selling home-brewed drinks; as inns, purpose-built or converted from other structures and licensed by the local Justices (or, pre-1552, even earlier authorities) to sell beer, wines and spirits to travellers (and offer overnight accommodation); or as taverns, normally selling just wine but not offering accommodation. (Colloquial names for ale and cider houses, licensed or unlicensed, were 'tippling houses', 'tiddleywinks' and 'tiddlywink houses'.) These theoretical distinctions by establishment and service were, however, usually blurred in practice. Then, with the passing of the Beer House Act in 1830 the number of licensed premises was greatly increased (from roughly 50,000 in 1828 to 82,500 three years later) for the Act permitted any householder to sell beer and cider to the public providing they paid just two guineas to the Excise for the necessary permit, the result being that many hitherto illegal drinking dens took the opportunity to become respectable (though many continued to break the law by selling wines and spirits under the counter).

A well-lit pub looks especially welcoming at night, as exemplified here by Ye Olde Anchor Inn at Upton-upon-Severn.

Almost always the beer would be brewed on the premises – often by the licensee's wife, or 'alewife', since time immemorial – and sold in the front room of their farm or townhouse thereby making it literally a 'public alehouse' (soon shortened to 'public house' or 'pub'). This arrangement was often intended merely to provide a second income for the household, with the licensee retaining his previous occupation – often reflected in the pub's name – unless it proved so successful a venture that he became a full-time landlord (and apply for a full publican's licence). Later amendments to the law though meant that by 1872 the local Justices were in control of all licensed premises.

Inside – unless they were the most simple of one-room establishments – most pubs had a hierarchical room structure. Prices were lowest in the 'public bar' – and the fixtures and fittings the plainest: bare wooden or stone floors, wooden seats, wooden and/or cast-iron tables. (In the roughest establishments, empty beer barrels sufficed.) This was where agricultural labourers and manual workers fresh from the factory or foundry would drink; women were actively discouraged from entering (unless of a certain profession), or even barred completely. Next up the scale were the 'snug' and the 'smoke room': smaller, more intimate areas, usually with a serving hatch rather than a bar counter, where private conversations could be held and business deals transacted. Often the snug was the wives' domain while their husbands drank in the public bar. At the top was the 'lounge' or 'saloon bar': carpeted, with upholstered seats, pictures on the wall, its own bar (often with table service) and higher prices. During the latter half of the nineteenth century brewers would compete as to who could provide the most luxurious of rooms and so attract the others' customers. Sometimes this air of opulence would be permitted to engulf the whole pub, with large and ornate mirrors everywhere, coloured glass lampshades over the gas mantles, bold-patterned, red wallpaper on the walls, and heavy dark wood and brass fittings abounding. Sadly, few of these remarkable 'gin palaces' survive unaltered today, and then only in the larger towns and cities.

During the 1960s and '70s there was a regrettable craze for removing internal walls and turning multi-room pubs into cavernous spaces, usually with a central island bar, all supposedly in the name of modernisation but really in order to pack in as many drinkers as possible. Thankfully that fad has more or less passed, though in too many instances the damage has been done – a major reason why many otherwise excellent pubs have been excluded from this book.

By the end of the nineteenth century a brewing revolution had taken place. The sheer number of local outlets for beer (it is no exaggeration to say that in many towns and cities there was a pub on every other street corner) meant that brewing on a large-scale became an extremely profitable enterprise, with a single, purpose-built brewery supplying as many pubs as it could within an area served by a horse and dray. As in any other business of this kind, brewers competed fiercely with each other, leading to a process of amalgamation and takeover that is still going on today. The result was the increasing dominance of a mere handful of brewing companies, assisted by the spread of the railway network and the rise of commercial motor transport, on first a local, then a regional, and finally a national scale.

Above all, a good pub must have cheery, welcoming staff, as here at the Coach & Horses Inn, Weatheroak Hill. The bigger the display of beer mats and pump clips in a pub the better, for it is a sign that the task of providing as broad a range of beers as possible is taken very seriously indeed.

Before this revolution in the trade, all pubs would normally have been owned, or rented from a local landowner, by the publican. With the rise of the large commercial brewer, many of them were bought up by the breweries to become 'tied houses' run by a tenant landlord or a manager, thus guaranteeing them outlets for their increasingly characterless products. Consumers' choice of what beers they could find in their local became more and more limited while at the same time the pubs themselves lost much of their character at the hands of these new, faceless conglomerates more concerned with brand image, corporate awareness and making every pub they owned look like every other pub they owned, from the signage outside to the carpets inside. Those that remained free of the tie became known as 'free houses' – a decreasingly small number in total.

The next major change came in 1989 when, under the Government's Beer Orders, breweries were required to limit the size of their tied estate. The result was that many tied pubs were sold to 'pubcos' – companies owning a large chain of up to several thousand pubs – or that brewers simply gave up brewing to become pubcos themselves; a few were sold to their tenant landlords. Although the Beer Orders were rescinded in 2003, the change had become more or less permanent and the pubcos were here to stay. The free house was rapidly becoming a thing of the past.

In 1971, however, concerned consumers began to fight back with the formation of the Campaign for Real Ale – better known as CAMRA. This pressure group is dedicated to encouraging the production and appreciation of 'real ale': that is, living, cask-conditioned beer rather than sterile, industrially produced keg beers and lagers – and to publicising and applauding the efforts of a new generation of small-scale local brewers and the landlords who stock their products. So successful has CAMRA been in changing public perception of what good beer is, that the wheel has turned full circle and today a growing number of the county's pubs are once more brewing their own beer.

Sadly, pubs are still closing, especially in rural areas, casualties of a combination of changing social habits, increasing overheads and stricter drink-driving laws, though many local authorities seem to have woken up to the fact that a pub is an essential part of village life and, when one closes, so part of the village dies with it. Consequently, approval for a change of use – to higher-value residential premises, for example – is thankfully less likely to be given than was once the case. It has been estimated by CAMRA (February 2007) that an average of fifty-six pubs close every month in the UK – and, more crucially, it is believed that for the first time since the Norman Conquest more than half our villages are 'dry'. (New pubs and bars opening reduce the overall loss by half, but this in no way compensates for the damage done to the social cohesion of the affected communities.) Our own experience while researching this book bears this out: the majority of villages in Worcestershire now have no pub, and the initials PH on a two-year-old map or road atlas are no guarantee that that pub will still be open. In our home town of Kidderminster, we have seen pubs shutting at the rate of one per year during the last ten years or so, continuing a trend that has been going on since the late nineteenth century at least. Obviously, this trend cannot continue indefinitely – the question is, when will it stop? A glimmer of hope is provided by our discovery that, while talking to pub regulars during research trips, a growing number of the 25–35 age group are tiring of the noisy, crowded, vertical-drinking bars in the town centres and venturing out to appreciate the joys of the more leisurely social interaction afforded by a traditional community pub – though what effect the 2007 smoking ban will have remains to be seen.

The key to a pub's survival lies in making it attractive to customers – and with a pub with some age and character to it, what better place to start than that? Astonishingly, there seems to have been no end to the continuing spoilation of historic buildings by the removal of internal walls, covering of original floors with inappropriate carpets and packing it full of dreary brown tables to turn the place into what is, in truth, nothing more than an up-market canteen designed to operate for the convenience of the staff, not the clientele. Gone is the intimate atmosphere

The old and the new: three bottled beers from the Talbot Hotel at Knightwick, one of Worcestershire's four modern, pub-based micro-breweries, and a drinks tray from the largest supplier of beer to the county, Marston's. Before February 2007 this concern was Wolverhampton & Dudley Breweries, formed in 1890 as Banks's. The tray is embossed with the names of both Banks's (the Wolverhampton brewery) and Hanson's (the one in Dudley, acquired in 1943 but closed in 1991).

engendered by separate rooms, serving hatches and cosy fireside corners, lost is any sense of tradition and history – and all too often at the hands of brewers who promote themselves and their products by appealing to that very tradition and history. It has to be said that a great many of the pubs we visited hide their history only too well: Tudor partitions removed, Georgian brickwork pebbledashed, Victorian walls and ceilings encrusted with inappropriate paints and papers, beautiful original floors carpeted over, fake 'beams' stuck onto plasterwork, and brass nick-nacks, tin swords and prints of the Italian Lakes hung everywhere. Outside, garish signs, cheap plastic furniture and acres of concrete slabs do little to entice in passers-by. Original Elizabethan or Victorian fixtures and fittings do not date, 1970s or 1990s makeovers most certainly do.

Worcestershire is blessed in its number of excellent pubs, so how then have the pubs included here been selected? At first glance it may seem that some of the pubs included are somewhat odd choices – the youngest building, for example, is little more than twenty years old while the most recent conversion to a pub described here dates from 2002 – but they are not. Indeed, strict criteria have been used to measure whether or not a pub justifies consideration for inclusion in the first place, and age was not one of them. (Sadly, being the oldest pub in a town or village is no guarantee of excellence.) To begin with, they must be pubs lying within the current county boundary – that is, not hotels whose prime purpose is to provide accommodation, nor eateries with no separate public bar where the provision of meals takes precedence over the sale of drink, nor town centre one-room bars with no sense of history or community to them. These establishments may be good at what they do – but they are not pubs. (Note that through the vagaries of history, many pubs though entitled 'The —Hotel' nowadays offer no accommodation at all. Similarly, a former pub might well retain its old name – and even traditional sign – but in essence be little more than a restaurant or bistro. Or, in one bizarre instance, a hire-car office!) Many pubs do of course serve food – as pubs have always done – but as part of the total service, not as their primary function. Interestingly, several pubs are now diversifying into foreign, more exotic cuisines – and even takeaways – in order to attract customers.

Secondly, they must sell real ale – that is, living, breathing, cask-conditioned beer of a consistently high quality. (The only exception to this rule is the Cider House at Defford, which sells real cider and no beer at all. Let it not be forgotten that Worcestershire is most definitely a cider county, which, along with its fellow beverage, perry, is enjoying a welcome upturn in fortune in recent years after many decades of decline.)

Thirdly, they must display in their structure and fittings features reflecting their history, and have not been altered beyond all recognition into those twin horrors of our time, the 'theme bar' and its pretentious sibling, the 'gastropub'. Traditional pub games, open fires and community noticeboards are welcome bonuses.

Finally, they must be well-run and welcoming, with friendly staff and a congenial atmosphere – and consequently be recommended by us. In short, they are places where one could gladly while away an afternoon or evening over a drink or two, and even a meal – not places where you are expected to sit down, eat up and get out.

The entries are not intended to be year by year, licensee by licensee accounts of each individual pub – for reasons of space, for one thing, and because early records are incomplete or missing for another – but rather snapshots capturing a taste of the building's history, and the flavour of its atmosphere today, in both words and pictures. So that like can be compared with like, the pubs have been grouped by function into the following categories: riverside, wayside, canalside and railway, local, and brew pubs.

One further point needs to be made for the benefit of readers wishing to sample the delights of any or all of the establishments mentioned here. Recent changes in the English licensing laws to allow for extended opening hours – the so-called '24-hour drinking' – have had, in many places, exactly the opposite effect. Pubs are no longer obliged to open a certain number of hours every day and consequently many publicans choose not to open until late afternoon or evening on weekdays; some are shut for one or two days entirely. Anyone intending to visit an unfamiliar pub listed here is strongly advised to telephone first to ascertain times of opening. The relevant telephone number is given at the head of each entry, as are website addresses (if applicable) where details of accommodation offered, forthcoming special events and so on can be checked. Also given are the pubs' postcodes for the benefit of motorists using satellite navigation devices, and basic directions for walkers and drivers without them.

Finally, unless credited otherwise, all photographs are by Jan Dobrzynski; all were taken before the 2007 smoking ban came into force, so marking the end of an era in English pub history.

> When you have lost your inns drown your empty selves, for you will have lost the last of England.
>
> Hilaire Belloc, *This and That*, 'On Inns'

IN MEMORIAM
The much-loved New Inn, Cutnall Green
Closed 2007
Last landlord: long-time Worcestershire publican
John Skett

ONE

Mug Houses

Free to sit and free to think,
Free to pay for what you drink.
Free to stop an hour or so,
When uneasy, free to go.

From a 1930s leaflet produced by J. Trow,
landlord of the Mug House, Claines

For countless centuries, from prehistoric times to the early decades of the Industrial Revolution, the main arterial thoroughfare for trade and transport in Worcestershire was the River Severn. This great waterway, the longest in Great Britain, runs the entire length of the county from north to south, entering it a little above Bewdley and leaving it just below Upton-upon-Severn.

Before the rivers of Britain, both large and small, were – literally – bypassed first by the canal, then the railway and the modern road networks, they provided the means whereby goods and people could be moved around the country – often in association with coastal shipping. They were, in the absence of proper roads, after those left by the Romans were allowed to fall into disrepair, quite simply the major transport highways of their day. Consequently, a whole range of service and other industries established themselves at convenient points along them – usually at the site of fords or bridges – to supply the wants of those using the river, and of their rowed, towed or sailed craft.

So the riverside inn came into being. Not really a hotel – for riverfolk slept on their boats – it offered food, entertainment and, above all, drink to its passing, water-borne customers. The Severn, as befitting its status as Britain's premier river, is lined at regular intervals with such pubs, survivors of probably twice as many along its banks at one time or another. In Worcestershire (and in Shropshire to the north) they go by the generic title of 'mug houses', the origins of which curious epithet lie in the pottery-producing region of the Ironbridge Gorge in Shropshire: crude earthenware beer mugs produced there were much-favoured by landlords along the river, probably for their low replacement cost if damaged or stolen by passing boatmen compared to expensive glass or pewter ones, and the name stuck, so much so that it was even adopted as a pub's official name by serveral of them. (Elsewhere

The recurrent hazard faced by every mug house: flooding. This is the Swan Hotel at Upton-upon-Severn at the beginning of 2007, with the town's temporary flood barrier erected.

in Britain the continuing use of the word 'pot', as in 'pint pot', harks back to the use of similar pottery mugs.)

Today almost all commercial traffic has vanished from the Worcestershire Severn, though a number of splendid mug houses survive, relying now for their trade on passing leisure boats and motorists.

The Severn's tributary, the Avon, is included at the end of this chapter. While never having the same commercial importance as the Severn, the river has long been an important navigable waterway and, as such, had its own mug houses.

On the Severn

BEWDLEY: *MUG HOUSE*

12 Severn Side North, Bewdley, DY12 2EE · 01299 402543 ·
www.mughousebewdley.co.uk

No parking. Access on foot from one of the nearby public car parks

The first town encountered by the Severn in Worcestershire is Bewdley, once a thriving port and centre for a myriad of small, now long-gone industries. Today it is a popular tourist spot, a consequence of its attractive riverside appearance, its proximity to Birmingham and its location on the Severn Valley Railway preserved steam line. Its principal quaysides are on the west bank of the river, divided by Thomas Telford's stone road bridge of the 1790s into Severn Side North and Severn Side South. The name derives from the old French *beau lieu*, or 'beautiful place'.

The Mug House, Bewdley.

Previously known as Coals Quay from the principal commodity transshipped here from waggons bringing it down from the small pits scattered along the western side of the river to the north, Severn Side North was once home to four pubs, of which only two survive today. Midway along the quayside stands the fittingly-named Mug House, which dates back – as a pub – to at least 1808. The first recorded licensee was John Smith, in 1831, whose occupation was given as 'waterman'; in 1861 the licensee was Henry Southan, a 'lantern leaf maker' and for much of the remainder of the nineteenth century the pub was run by one member or another of the Southan family. (Lantern leaves, or translucent panes, were made from thin sheets of flattened horn, as were combs and other domestic items. The manufacturer of such commodities was a significant industry in the town – there was even a Comb Maker's Arms in the High Street.)

At the start of the eighteenth century the Severn could be comfortably navigated up into Shropshire but by the nineteenth century going beyond Bewdley was not so easy with shallows and rock bars presenting serious obstacles to shipping, especially

during the drier seasons. For that reason the Bewdley mug houses were where teams of hardy, casual labourers known as bow-hauliers were hired to tow boats upstream. The standard rate of pay was 2s 6d per day, plus two meals and two mugs of ale – hence the expression, 'to be had for a mug'. To haul a boat the 15 miles from Bewdley to Bridgnorth took up to twenty men, depending upon the condition of the river, the weather and so on. (On the underside of Thomas Telford's bridge, just below the Mug House can be seen the marks worn by the bow-hauliers' ropes.) Finally nature won out and today the river is navigable only by the shallowest of rowing boats.

The Mug House – sometimes known as the Old Mug House – brewed its own beer until at least 1900 but by 1903 it was owned by the Worcestershire Brewing & Malting Co. Ltd, along with several other of the town's pubs. This concern had been formed in 1898 by the merger of Bucknells of Kidderminster and the Delph Brewery of Brierley Hill in the Black Country. It eventually built up an estate of more than 120 pubs, changing its name in 1906 to the Kidderminster Brewing Co. Ltd before being taken over seven years later by Wolverhampton & Dudley Breweries, marketed as Banks's after

The Mug House's one bar.

its Wolverhampton brewery. (This long-familiar West Midlands name is now vanishing from its hundreds of pub signs, the company being rebranded in February 2007 as Marston's after the Burton-upon-Trent brewer it swallowed in 1999.)

The pub has experienced several changes of fortune since then, including the removal of internal walls and the addition of false beams and modern brickwork, but has recently enjoyed a marked upswing in its fortunes under a new owner since 2003 as a traditional small pub serving quality food in the dining area, the Angry Chef Restaurant in what was once a separate building next door, which can be acessed from the pub. A popular annual beer festival is held in the spring and bed and breakfast accommodation is also offered. In 2006 it was voted the best inn in the area for both food and drink. Thankfully, in 2003/4 a demountable flood barrier was installed along the quayside to protect the pub and its neighbours from the Severn's regular and increasingly frequent bursting of its banks here.

The source-to-mouth long-distance footpath known as the Severn Way passes on the other side of the river from the Mug House, with Bewdley station on the preserved Severn Valley Railway five minutes' walk beyond that; the much shorter Worcestershire Way runs directly outside the pub.

STOURPORT-ON-SEVERN: *ANGEL INN*

14 Severn Side, Stourport-on-Severn, DY10 2PY · 01299 822661

Access via Severn Road from Mitton Lane, or Mart Lane from Low Hill, off the one-way town centre system

Set back from, and facing the Severn in proper mug house-fashion, the Angel is quite possibly the oldest pub in Stourport. The town owes its origin to the coming of the Staffordshire & Worcestershire Canal in 1772 (see Chapter 3) and the Angel is thought to have been in existence by 1780, as the Virgins Inn. This pub in turn gave its name to the land upon which it stood, by the mouth of the River Stour: Virgins Inn Close. Sometime later the pub took its present name and, if it is not the earliest, it is probably – along with the Black Star (see Chapter 3) – one of the two oldest surviving pubs in the town.

The Angel Inn, Stourport-on-Severn.

The riverside beside the Angel Inn.

In the public bar.

The first recorded licensee was John Stringer, who was there from before 1820 to 1828; he was succeeded by his wife Penelope and her second husband Samuel Cole, then by his son James Stringer (1868–84) – a typical example of a pub staying with one family for half a century or more during the Victorian era. During the Edwardian era the licensee was one Captain Henry 'Harry' Hatton, who operated a small fleet of pleasure steamers from the pub. ('Captain' was probably an honorary title.) By this date the Severn was no longer navigable above Stourport but between there and Worcester a thriving steamer trade had sprung up to help fill the gap left in the local economy by the demise of freight traffic.

The Angel has been much altered over the years, with the lighter brickwork and inwards slope of the outside walls suggesting that the third storey to the building was added at a later (probably early nineteenth century) date. Traces of what are thought to have been a gents' toilet and a smokehouse for smoking bacon are visible on the south end wall – the pub dating from a time when many housholds regularly kept a pig or two, the meat from which they (or a neighbour) would smoke for eating throughout the winter. A curious iron attachment to the front wall probably held a burning torch to help guide passers-by to the pub in the days before street lighting, and to light the landing place of the ferry that once crossed the river here. In 2002 however, a great deal of the pub's atmosphere was lost when the downstairs area was drastically remodelled, though enough remains to justify the pub's inclusion in this book and it is likely that the brashness of the refurbishment will be mellowed by time. The whole building rises gently up the slope away from the river with a small public bar on one side of the entrance corridor and a larger 'Little Cottage Lounge' dining room on the other; this latter room can be booked for functions. Accommodation is also available.

Sadly, the Angel's upstream neighbour, the grand and impressive Tontine, built by the Canal Company in 1773 as the Areley Inn, not only to serve merchants and traders on both waterways (and provide them with accommodation) but also to house its own offices and boardroom – and a ballroom! – is no longer open. It was closed in 2001 after several years of neglect and at the time of writing is likely to be converted into luxury apartments.

The Severn Way runs directly in front of both establishments on its way downstream.

GRIMLEY: *CAMP HOUSE INN*

Camp Lane, Grimley Village, Worcester, WR2 6LX · 01905 640288

Take either of the two turnings for Grimley east off the A443 midway between Worcester and Ombersley, then turn right at the entrance to the village and follow the lane (about 1 mile in all)

This ancient, cream-painted pub has long been a mug house, and is perhaps the most pleasantly-situated of all those on the Severn, located as it is in completely rural surroundings on the west bank of the river just below Bevere (or Camp) Island. It was licensed by Oliver Cromwell after the Battle of Worcester in 1651 and was for several centuries the site of a punt ferry across the Severn. There was a rocky bar across the Severn close by, which occasioned great delays to traffic when the river was low – on which occasions the Camp House profited greatly from the waiting boatmen! The pub was also witness to a serious accident in 1715 when, on 13 September, a wherry from Shrewsbury was in collision with a barge and six people lost their lives.

During the late Georgian period an adjacent meadow was used as a racecourse with the local squire, Richard Griffiths of Thorngrove, acting as organiser and steward. However, as is not unknown to happen in the world of the turf, in 1834 trouble arose over some horses he ran and he withdrew his financial support, thus putting an end to the meetings. A framed 1834 racecard can be seen in the pub's taproom while also displayed is a reprinted account of an 1833 meeting (reproduced on p. 12).

The Camp House Inn, Grimley, in its tranquil setting by the Severn.

One of the Camp House's resident peacocks.

The Camp House later gained much trade in late Victorian and Edwardian times arising from the popularity of the island and its surroundings as a beauty spot, frequented as it was by summer strollers and pleasure steamer passengers from Worcester; afternoon teas were served as well as the more customary stronger beverages. (The ferry, enabling walkers on one bank to cross to the other and so do a 'round trip' from the city, operated until the 1930s.) The inn takes its name from Bevere Island's rather less happy use as a camp by the citizens of Worcester fleeing the city to escape the ravages of war or – for the last time in 1637 – the plague. The island is named after the beaver, once native to these shores but long since hunted to extinction for its fur, while Grimley probably derives from an Anglo-Saxon personal name.

Inside, the Camp House is a comparatively untouched, multi-room establishment full of old-world charm. Despite its isolation it is very much a popular community pub where good food and drink can be enjoyed – especially outside in the summer. It is also well-frequented by bird watchers (as the displays on the wall attest), with a major viewing site in old gravel pits close by. The Severn Way passes the Camp House along the river bank, making it the perfect stopping-off point for walkers, who can sit beneath the trees and watch the river flow gently by – and admire the pub's peacocks in the garden.

Sometimes the river is not so gentle, and during the winter flooding in January 2007 Alan Wainwright, son of licensee Jim Wainwright, used a punt to ferry pub-goers to and from the higher-standing reaches of the lane. His reward? A pint of beer per trip – not at all bad, as he was reported as making up to forty trips a day!

A classic pub scene: a game of dominoes in full swing. A pub favourite since at least the beginning of the nineteenth century, the game was probably imported from the Continent in Tudor times and has spawned many variants here. Generally speaking, most parts of the country play with a 'pack' of twenty-eight 'bones', going up to double-six, though the set of fifty-five (going up to double-nine) has a stronghold in the Lancashire area. The player on the left is Alan Wainwright, son of the licensee, and some-time ferryman.

Another look at this wonderful inn.

Camp Races were held on Wednesday last. The lowest estimate of the company present gives the number at 2,000, and the day's recreation evidently afforded unalloyed enjoyment and satisfaction to all.

A spacious meadow on the banks of the Severn was, as usual, the scene of the sport, and rarely has this crack meeting been productive of a better day's diversion than on this occasion.

Some of the heats were admirably contested, more especially those between high-breed steeds which were admirably jockied by some young aspirants for equestrian fame.

The course, in the absence of Mr Tolley, was not particularly well kept, the consequence being one or two clumsy falls, but without producing any material injury either to riders or their steeds.

From the *Worcester Herald*, 1833

CLAINES: *MUG HOUSE*

Claines Lane, Claines, Worcester, WR3 7RN · 01905 456649

Coming from the north on the A449 Kidderminster to Worcester road, take the second exit at the Oak Farm roundabout (between the exits for the M5 and Worcester), then first right (Cornmeadow Lane). Parking is on the road

At first glance, the tiny village of Claines, just on the northern edge of the city of Worcester, is a curious place to find a mug house, located as it is several hundred yards from the River Severn. Whereas the Camp House at Grimley (with which the Mug House is almost level) is right on the Severn's western bank, the eastern bank is not so high and has the additional complication of the River Salwarpe coming in a little to the north, the result being a large, virtually uninhabited floodplain between Claines and the Severn. The pub also had the benefit of being on the old road between Worcester and Ombersley and points north. The name Claines is almost certainly a corruption of 'clay-ness', or 'the clay headland'.

The Mug House's principal claim to fame is that it is the only pub in England that stands inside a churchyard. The parish church, dedicated to St John the Baptist, dates from the fifteenth century (replacing an earlier structure) and it is thought the Mug House dates from at least that time – in 1934 it celebrated its 600th

The uniquely sited Mug House, Claines, from the graveyard.

Welcoming faces behind the bar.

anniversary though this date was probably picked more for publicity purposes than with any strict adherence to historical accuracy; it is certainly recorded as being in use in 1538 when vestry meetings were being held there. It is of course not unusual to find a pub in close proximity to a church, though in Claines it is carried to its limit. The reason is that both are age-old centres of community life – one religious, one secular – and both have a natural location at the heart of a village. Furthermore, the pub would often stand on land owned by the church while its brewery would supply the church for its 'church ales': fund-raising acitivities originally held in the churches themselves, then in churchyards, and finally (in some cases) in purpose-built breweries on church ground, often on the saint's day of the church's dedicatee and other major festivals. (One of these buildings existed at Caines: converted into almshouses in 1773, it was demolished in 1866.)

A regularly observed fixture on a parish church's calendar for many centuries was Rogationtide, in the week before Ascension Day (forty days after Easter). Then the coming corn harvest would be blessed, and the parish bounds beaten to the accompaniment of much drinking known as a 'heavy wet'. Again, the Mug House at Claines would have played its part to the full in these celebrations. Today a more sober religious connection continues with a Sunday School class being held in the pub, while the drinking tradition is upheld when the pub is used for wedding receptions, and christening and funeral gatherings – just as it always has been.

Inside the entrance hallway, with the back of the bar serving hatch on the left.

Pub mugs and jugs on display in the snug. Common pub ornaments, the mugs would have been used originally for beer and cider, and the jugs for water to add to whisky.

(During the 1950s the parson would lead his congregation to the pub after services – and claim a free pint.)

Inside the timber-framed brick building there is a very small public bar, an equally small snug and a larger lounge/dining area at the back with views towards Worcester and the Malvern Hills beyond (and a large mural depicting the pub in 1745). Outside, a number of tables between the pub and the graveyard provide the additional seating much needed on pleasant summer evenings, and are ideal vantage points from which to enjoy the regular visits of Morris Men – and to contemplate one's mortality!

In 1637 Worcester was ravaged by the plague and within twelve months some 1,500 people had died from it. Claines was not spared, forcing the Constable of Claines to order the closure of six pubs in the village the following year, prompting an anonymous writer at the time to record that 'Our poor are provided for, the highways repaired, riot we know none, gamesters we know none, drunkards and drunkenness none'.

The Mug House is said to be haunted by the ghosts of soldiers killed at the 1651 Battle of Worcester. One of these (or another ghost entirely) reportedly goes to the door, shouts 'Beware!' then walks to the church to play the organ. In the cellar, things are switched on and off, and glasses smashed on the floor.

In 1947 another, more tangible mystery was unearthed. After a storm damaged one of the pub's walls, repair work uncovered the silver head of a bishop's medieval crozier. Whether hidden to save it at the time of the Reformation, or simply stashed stolen property, it was presented to the Bishop of Worcester and is used once a year by the Claines Boy Bishop: during the period from St Nicholas' Day (6 November) to Holy Innocents Day (28 December) every year, a church choirboy acts as a member of the clergy. This widespread medieval custom, banned by Henry VIII, was revived in 1971 at Claines and continues to this day.

UPTON-UPON-SEVERN: SWAN HOTEL

Waterside, Upton-upon-Severn, WR8 0JD · 01684 592317

On the riverside street a short walk downstream from the A4104 road bridge over the Severn. Several public car parks close by

Upton-upon-Severn is a pleasant little market town situated on the higher, but still low-lying, western bank of the River Severn roughly midway between Worcester and Tewkesbury. Its name simply means 'the farm higher up (the Severn)'. In medieval times it was an important port but now relies on agriculture and tourism, the number of visitors swelled at regular intervals by the several annual festivals it is host to (many of them music-themed). In consequence, the town still has half a dozen or more thriving pubs, each tending to attract a different type of customer. Four of the pubs are sited on the river, testimony to the importance of the Severn in the past, and of the quartet the oldest is the seventeenth-century Swan (also recorded at times as the White Swan). This medium-sized pub and hotel is the furthest south of the four, and sits at a slightly higher level than the younger pubs upstream of it – the latter are consequently far more prone to flooding than the Swan; the builders in the olden days had far more respect for the river. That is not to say it is unaffected by the Severn's periodic overflowing, since when the modern temporary flood barriers are deployed access to the Swan is, ironically, cut off as well. The pub's cellar is also susceptible to flooding and indeed, at the time of going to publication, the Swan is closed for a complete refurbishment.

While the inside of the pub is not out of the ordinary, the outside certainly is. To begin with, the hotel and pub parts of the establishment are distinctly separate, with their own entrances; the pub portion comprises two oak-beamed bars (one with a log fire) and a restaurant area, this part being the original mug house – formed from three cottages and a blacksmith's shop – far older than the later nineteenth-century, fairly-ordinary hotel building set at right-angles to it. Tables are also provided outside for customers to enjoy the comings and goings of the river craft, either

The Swan Hotel at Upon-upon-Severn, behind its early 2007 flood barrier. The marooned pub half of the establishment is the low, narrow building on the right.

passing or using the waterside moorings. A converted outbuilding, the Barn Bar, which once was a warehouse, is available for use on special occasions.

The Severn Way, after crossing the river to the west bank by way of the town's one bridge, passes the Swan's front door.

While not a mug house in the true sense, the Little Upton Muggery at 58 Old Street, on the other side of the town from the river, is well worth a visit if only to view the astonishing collection of mugs of all shapes and sizes on display, a relic from the days when it was once part of Mad O'Rourke's Little Pub empire. (See the Little Pack Horse at Bewdley in Chapter 4.)

On the Avon

WYRE PIDDLE: *ANCHOR*

Main Road, Wyre Piddle, Pershore, WR10 2JB · 01386 556059 ·
www.anchorwyrepiddle.co.uk

Coming from Worcester on the A44 towards Evesham, pass the Pinvin and Pershore turn-offs then take the second exit at the Spion Kop roundabout and continue straight on into the village

The River Severn's major tributary in Worcestershire is the Avon, and after being opened up by William Sandys between 1636 and 1640 the river became an important navigable waterway in its own right. It enters the county from Warwickshire (where it is commonly known as Shakespeare's Avon to distinguish it from the two other English rivers of the same name) a little to the north of Evesham,

The Anchor, Wyre Piddle, on a Pershore-printed postcard posted in 1909. The scene is not so different today, especially since the village was bypassed. (*Author's collection*)

The Anchor's sign by the river – very much a necessity since several of the pub's customers arrive by water.

then meanders leisurely across the southernmost part of Worcestershire in a generally south-westerly direction before joining the Severn at Tewkesbury, just over the border in Gloucestershire.

Wyre Piddle is a small village on the north bank of the Avon north-west of Evesham, squeezed between it and the Piddle Brook. The 'Wyre' element of the name is obscure. The Anchor is an old, sprawling, half-timbered building sandwiched tightly between the village's main street and the river and, as its name suggests, was established as a pub to serve the passing river trade (now replaced by pleasure boaters). It probably dates from a century or so before the time of the navigation improvement with its situation on the main Evesham to Worcester road making it an ideal place to stop for refreshment. Inside, the Anchor is a relatively unspoilt multi-room building, incorporating a restaurant. Outside a large, terraced beer garden overlooks the river and the lower bank and fields beyond. It is now the only pub in the village, the other – the George Inn – having been converted into a private house.

Relaxing at the bar in the Anchor.

For much of the 1990s the Anchor was home to the Wyre Piddle Brewery, before it moved down the road to Pinvin. This is a bottle of its 3.9% Piddle in the Hole, beside a nineteenth-century strong ale glass.

The open space at the front of the pub was where the village's annual Wakes, or fair, was held.

Between 1992, when it was established by Martyn Wilkins (formerly a Stourbridge publican) and 2002, when it relocated to larger premises at Pinvin, the pub was home to the Wyre Piddle Brewery, the brewhouse being housed in an outbuilding.

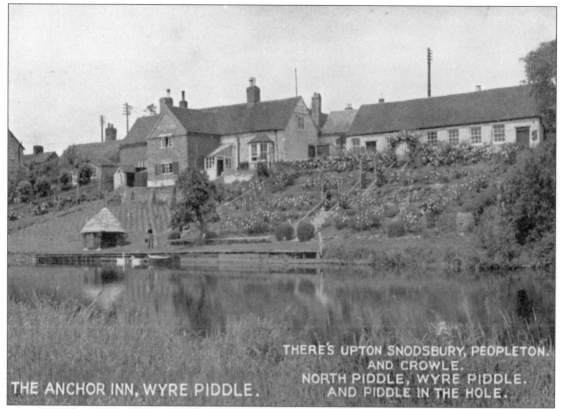

THERE'S UPTON SNODSBURY, PEOPLETON.
AND CROWLE.
NORTH PIDDLE, WYRE PIDDLE.
AND PIDDLE IN THE HOLE.

THE ANCHOR INN, WYRE PIDDLE.

The river frontage of the Anchor, on a slightly later, anonymously produced postcard. Again, the peaceful scene is not so different today. *(Author's collection)*

Here many beers were brewed, for sale in selected local outlets, the brand names used, such as Piddle in the Hole and Piddle in the Wind, taking their slightly cheeky inspiration from an age-old children's rhyme listing some place-names of the area:

There's Upton Snodsbury, Peopleton and Crowle
North Piddle, Wyre Piddle and Piddle in the Hole

TWO

Wayside Inns

As you chat and stand before the fire,
Pray sit down . . . 'tis my desire
That other folks as well as you,
May see the fire, and feel it too.
A notice displayed in the Claines Mug House leaflet , op. cit.

In one sense, the term 'wayside inn' applies to any hostelry sited beside a road. In practice however, it should be taken to mean a pub or inn whose primary reason for existence was to cater for highway travellers in much the same way as the mug houses served those on the river. Such travellers tended to be residents from the surrounding countryside, on foot, on horseback or in carts, on their way to market or carrying goods down to the river or canal for transshipment. Some would even be pilgrims, journeying – in the case of Worcestershire – to visit one of the several cathedrals or abbeys in the region. (With the Dissolution of the Monasteries in the 1550s, such great religious houses ceased to offer hospitality to travellers, meaning a rise in fortunes of lay establishments.)

The Fox Inn, Hanley Broadheath. The photograph conveys admirably the isolation of many wayside inns.

A great many wayside inns remain today along the rural highways and byways of Britain, often still characterised by their isolation from other dwellings for they were deliberately sited between towns and villages to enjoy a monopoly of the passing trade. Sometimes their name is a clue to their original purpose. Halfway House, for example, informed passers-by that they had reached the midway point of the journey between two towns. For many, that original purpose is the same today, though nowadays they are likely to have been extended to provide dining areas for modern travellers, the sale of drinks to a few locals not being sufficient to keep them in business. In some cases the provision of food has far overshadowed the sale of drink, and the building has evolved from a pub into an eatery where customers are often made to feel that they are part of an industrial process as soon as they enter: they are sat down, given a drink, given a meal – then given the boot. A pub should be a place in which to linger and savour the atmosphere, not a canteen and, as stated in the Introduction, such establishments are outside the scope of this book.

One particular variety of wayside inn could however be found in towns as well: the coaching inn. This term applies specifically to those far grander inns built (or re-established) for one principal purpose: to serve the coaching trade of Britain from the late Elizabethan times onwards. At first, only wealthy individuals and families could afford a carriage of any kind but, in the late seventeenth century, commercial operators began running stagecoaches over set routes to a fixed timetable, the journey being made in manageable stages from one coaching inn to another – hence the name. Such journeys were still expensive however and it was not until the railway boom of the 1850s and 1860s that cheap travel came within the reach of the masses, so spelling the end of the coaching inn. Designed especially to meet the needs of the coaching trade, these inns provided food, drink and lodgings for passengers, and the same for their drivers; in addition, they were where fresh horses could be supplied at the end of a stage, and provisions and stabling provided for the exhausted ones.

More so perhaps than any of the other type of pub featured in this book, the coaching inn's function had a great deal of influence on its structure and layout. Invariably built around a courtyard (to give protection from the weather and ease of access), the ground floor would encompass the stables plus drinking and dining areas, while the first floor would comprise private dining rooms for wealthier and more genteel clientele, and their bedrooms. A second or even third floor – often in the attic – would contain cheaper sleeping accommodation, and servants' quarters. The courtyard, at the heart of the building, would be large enough for a coach to be turned round in and accessed by an archway large enough for that coach to pass through. The first floor rooms would often give out onto a gallery, from which guests could watch a performance by strolling companies of players in the courtyard below, thus setting the architectural standard for later generations of playhouses and theatres.

Sadly, only a handful of coaching inns survive in anything like their original condition; the rest have fallen victim to changing fashions, property developers and road-widening schemes. Many though, survive in a much-altered state, including several in Worcestershire, either as simple locals or hotels proper with traces of their unique history only visible to those who know what to look for.

CLIFTON-UPON-TEME: *NEW INN*

Old Road, Clifton-upon-Teme, WR6 6DR · 01886 812226

Turn right off the B4204 Worcester to Tenbury Wells Road just before reaching Clifton and the pub is on the left

Located halfway up Clifton Hill, on the old road between the River Teme and the hilltop village of Clifton-upon-Teme (see Chapter 4), stands the former farm building that is the New Inn. In the nineteenth century this was a cider and ale house run by the Griffiths family; known as Shortlands, it later became the New Inn. Now bypassed by the B4204, it is extremely well hidden from the new road and the turn-off leading to it should be approached with care by motorists.

As was the custom in eighteenth- and nineteenth-century rural communities, the publican was almost always a farmer as well, and this was the case here. It is still noted for its real, locally-produced cider.

From the outside, it is clear that the pub has been enlarged over the decades, either with new extensions or by the incorporation of existing buildings, as has often been the case as increasing demands mean that the public part of the premises expands at the expense of the private. Inside, there is one large bar area plus a recently refurbished restaurant. For many years the New Inn has been the New

The New Inn, Clifton-upon-Teme.

Looking from the New Inn, past the sign on Old Road, to the ridge hiding the River Teme and Homme Castle. This typical view onto open countryside is an obvious reminder of the very rural nature of wayside inns.

A friendly welcome – and the locally produced cider is strongly recommended.

Year's Day meeting point for the Clifton Hunt which, founded in 1926, is one of the youngest hunts in England. It is also popular with ramblers and shooting parties, being a proper country pub in all respects.

Like the Bridge at Stanford Bridge (see Chapter 4), the New Inn also has strong connections with Shelsley Walsh immediately to the north, with many competitors and spectators drinking here over the years.

DUNHAMPSTEAD: *FIR TREE INN*

Trench Lane, Dunhampstead, WR9 7JX · 01905 774094 ·
www.firtreeinn.co.uk

Head south towards Worcester on the A38 from the A38 Roman Way/B4090
Worcester Road island south of Droitwich, then first left into Pulley Lane. Cross
Newland Road, first right into Tagwell Road, pass under the M5 then first left,
first right into Trench Lane

This extremely well-presented and recently refurbished wayside inn stands in the middle of a maze of country lanes a little way south of the village of Dunhampstead (or 'the hamstede on the hill'), sandwiched between the Worcester & Birmingham Canal to the west and the Bromsgrove to Cheltenham main railway line to the east. The building dates back to the late eighteenth century at least and was originally a drovers' inn, providing food, drink and shelter to that hardy breed of men who drove cattle halfway across the country from the Welsh Marches, where they had been fattened for the journey, to London (or other cities) for sale. It was a centuries-old trade, and over the years it became the custom that a fir tree or two would be planted by inns on the drove roads to act as markers – hence the pub's name, a modern variant of the original Firs Inn. (Interestingly, this was a custom perpetuated in the nineteenth century by the Great Western Railway, which did exactly the same to mark the location of its stations, town as well as rural.)

Outside, the Fir Tree boasts a heated patio and decking area for summer use; inside there is a long, multi-level bar plus a separate restaurant. The drinking area at the

The Fir Tree Inn, Dunhampstead.

The dining area . . .

. . . and the bar – and another
friendly welcome.

opposite end to the restaurant is known as the Murderers' Bar – a reference to a
notoriously infamous episode in the pub's history, the story of which is told in framed
cuttings from *Berrow's Worcester Journal* on the walls. Half a mile or so to the south-
east of the pub lies the village of Oddingley where, on Midsummer Day 1806, the local
parson the Revd George Parker was shot while out walking, then clubbed to death
with the gun butt by a Droitwich carpenter by the name of Richard Hemming (and
who was recognised by witnesses). Hemming made off, then promptly disappeared; in
1830 however, his skeleton – with the skull smashed in – was found by his brother-in-
law, Charles Burton, hidden in a barn on the nearby Netherton Farm. At last the
sordid truth began to emerge from the resulting confessions and accusations: a group
of local farmers led by one Captain Evans, in dispute with George Parker over the
matter of tithes, had arranged for Hemming to perform the dirty deed – and then
murdered him in turn. Evans had died in 1829 but three co-conspirators were tried
for various offences, though all were cleared. One of the three, Thomas Clewes, a
previous occupant of Netherton Farm and who had given evidence against the others,
appears to have been the most unwilling of the gang; he later took over the tenancy of
the Fir Tree though he was always reluctant to discuss the whole grisly affair and was
guarded from inquisitive strangers by his daughter in his final years of ill-health.

Parker's murder is said to have been planned at the Speed the Plough pub in
Tibberton, a village a couple of miles to the south.

HADLEY HEATH: *HADLEY BOWLING GREEN INN*

Copcut Lane, Hadley Heath, WR9 0AR · 01905 620294 ·
www.hadleybowlinggreen.com

Take the A4133 east off the A449 at Ombersley, or west off the A38
Roman Way at Droitwich. Go south at the crossroads in Hadley, then left
at the T-junction into Copcut Lane

Tucked away off a country lane midway between Droitwich to the east and the A449 to the west, and a little to the north of the Droitwich Canal, the Hadley Bowling Green Inn is one of Worcestershire's hidden gems. The building, originally a farm-cum-ale house belonging to Lord Sandys' estate, dates back to the latter half of the sixteenth century and is thought to have always had its bowling green and associated club (though the latter's records survive from 1775 only). As such, it is the oldest bowling green in the country and deservedly famous within bowling circles; technically, it is a crown or 'hog's back' green, as opposed to the flat greens favoured to the south of the Midlands. Visitors are encouraged to try their hand during the summer season – bowls are provided – though in earlier times the club was very much the preserve of the country gentry and nobility. During the eighteenth century the club had its own elaborate code of rules, rites and etiquette: swearing on the green resulted in a fine of 2s, with the money going to the poor of the parish, while 'If a member fails to pay his debts, the servant of the green shall

The Hadley Bowling Green Inn, Hadley Heath, from the edge of the historic bowling green.

One of the very well-appointed dining areas.

drag him on his breeches across the green'. As was the custom among the beaus and bucks of the day, heavy wagers were laid on matches.

For others of a different inclination, a rather more modern facility (being adopted by several rural pubs) is offered, namely a clay pigeon shooting ground.

The Bowling Green Inn's second principal claim to fame is that Guy Fawkes is said to have spent time here during the summer of 1604, with his fellow conspirators, hatching plans for what was to become known as the Gunpowder Plot – their attempt to blow up James I and Parliament that 5 November was foiled at the very last hour. By this date the establishment had risen somewhat in status to become a coaching inn. Then, or sometime later, it was also being used as a labour exchange of sorts, as were many pubs, village greens, town squares and other community focuses; these Mop Fairs, as they were termed, were so called because workers putting themselves out for hire for the coming year would hold an appropriate tool of their trade. (See accompanying quote.)

Ancient in appearance outside, the interior of the pub has been refurbished in a modern, refined but very sympathetic manner with a number of secluded areas for wining and dining as well as traditional beer drinking.

Notice is hereby given that at Hadley Bowling Green, in the Parish of Ombersley on Monday the 27th September, and on Monday the 4th of October, 1773, will be held A MOP for the Hiring of Servants. And the same will be continued every Year on the Monday before, and on the Monday after Michaelmas Day [29 September].

From a leaflet found in an Ombersley chimney stack

HANLEY BROADHEATH: *FOX INN*

Hanley Broadheath, Nr Tenbury Wells, WR15 8QS · 01886 853189 · www.foxinn-broadheath.co.uk

By the Herefordshire border on the B4204 Worcester to Tenbury Wells Road

Sited next to the boundary with Herefordshire where that county makes a large incursion into the far western arm of Worcestershire, the Fox Inn is a late sixteenth- or early seventeenth-century oak-framed building with a traditional black and white façade and later brick walls elsewhere. Grade II listed, the pub began life as a farmhouse and, as was so often the case with rural hostelries, successive landlords had second jobs as farmers until the end of the nineteenth century.

As a pub, the Fox has always been a privately owned freehouse and, as one would expect, has been subject to a number of additions and alterations over the years as the public space has encroached upon the private, the end result being a large but surprisingly cosy multi-roomed, multi-level establishment, complete with log fires. Since the current landlord took over in 2002, part of the building has been

The Fox Inn, Hanley Broadheath, from New Road.

The warm, fireplace
end of the long bar.

converted into the Phannipa Thai Restaurant though not, as has so often been the
case elsewhere, at the expense of the traditional pub atmosphere. Although sited in a
sparsely-populated landscape – most of the surrounding habitations are working
farms – the pub is very much a centre of its rural community, attracting drinkers
and diners from a wide catchment area. One notable special attraction, held at the
end of August each year, is a lawnmower-racing meeting in the field behind the pub;
another is an annual summer music and dance festival.

The pub's name is an obvious reference to the practice of fox hunting, traditional
to this area.

PENSAX: *BELL*

The Bell at Pensax, Abberley, WR6 6AE · 01299 896677

On the B4202 Clows Top Road between Abberley and Clows Top

Located roughly midway along the B4202 connecting the A456 at Clows Top and the A443 at Abberley south-west of Stourport-on-Severn, and some way from the village of Pensax, the Bell is the perfect example of what a wayside inn should be. A free house serving a range of real ales, cider and perry from regional breweries, and home-cooked food using local produce, the framed certificates on the walls testify to the many awards the pub has won – including CAMRA's West Midlands Pub of the Year in 2003 and Herefordshire & Worcestershire Pub of the Year in 2002, 2003 and 2004.

The present pub dates back to 1883, when an older, early nineteenth-century inn was rebuilt. The name is a fairly common pub name linking the building to a nearby religious establishment of some kind – in this case the Norman St James' Chapel, demolished in 1829 and rebuilt as the parish church three years later. It should be remembered that a bell, controlled by a religious establishment of some kind or other, was for many centuries the only way villagers in the fields could tell the exact hour before clocks became commonplace – and the very word 'clock', from the medieval English clokke, literally means bell, as does the French *cloche*.

The main bar, complete with early-evening regulars.

The Bell, Pensax, with one of its two signs: a real bell, cast at Loughborough in 1886. A century or more ago, when illiteracy was commonplace, a painted image – or even, as here, a solid object – served to advertise the presence of a pub far more effectively than a lettered sign.

Pensax was once a coal-mining village, though the last small pits closed after the Second World War; also gone are the village's other three pubs. The origins of the village's curious name are unknown, but date back to at least medieval times. As was the norm, the Bell's nineteenth-century landlords had various other jobs on the side, mining and farming being the two common ones here – the original pub's name was in fact the Hill o' Pits.

The tiny bar counter in the entrance hall: landlord John Greaves enjoys a quiet moment with John from the King & Castle, Kidderminster.

The Bell's other, more prosaic sign.   Relaxing by the fire in the snug.

In layout the Bell retains its original central hallway, complete with its own little bar counter, off which are a large bar, a cosy snug, and a corridor with an unusual glass-panelled wall leading to a small dining room. A range of pub- and brewery-related objects decorate the walls, and the furniture is old and worn – just as it should be. There are beer gardens front and back. With very few residents in its immediate vicinity, the Bell relies almost entirely on customers walking or driving from elsewhere; such is its reputation for good beer and a warm welcome, it has a dedicated and appreciative clientele only too willing to make the journey – especially when the pub is host to one of its regular beer festivals.

THREE

Canal & Railway Pubs

2 Pints make	1 Quart
4 Quarts make	1 Gallon
2 Gallons make	1 Argument
1 Argument makes	1 Quarrel
1 Quarrel makes	1 Fight
1 Fight makes	2 Policemen
1 Magistrate	make 20 Shillings
1 Magistrate's Clerk	or
1 Policeman	14 days

From the Claines Mug House leaflet op. cit.

During the last quarter of the eighteenth century what is now termed the Industrial Revolution went hand-in-glove with the beginning of Britain's Canal Age, resulting in a network of man-made waterways criss-crossing the country. They transported raw materials and finished products between mines and factories, ports and burgeoning cities. Consequently, just as had happened on the coach routes, canalside inns sprang up – sometimes not even accessible by road – to serve a new group of workers on their thousands of barges and narrowboats.

Half a century later, during the Railway Age of the 1840s and 1850s, history repeated itself, this time as a network of rails spread rapidly across the country linking virtually every town and city in the land – and a great many villages into the bargain. Ordinary people could, for the first time, travel quickly and cheaply over long distances, and the railway pubs beside every station assured passengers that they could secure refreshment and a good night's rest at the end of their journey if they needed it.

The coming of the railways led to a slow, inexorable decline in the fortunes of the canals – a decline hastened by the rise of the competing motor lorry. By the 1950s many had been closed – officially or by virtue of simply having fallen into disuse, their locks broken and tunnels impassable. Then, almost when it was too late, those who cared about these historic waterways literally muscled-in on the action, restoring and reopening derelict stretches at an outstanding rate, all for the benefit of a new generation of boat people keen to explore Britain's waterways just

The perfect setting for a railway pub: Kidderminster Town station concourse under its newly erected canopy, with the King & Castle in the far right corner.

for the simple pleasure of doing so – and by doing so, breathing new life into the canalside pubs.

The railway system too has had its bleak moments, notably during the notorious Dr Beeching era of the 1960s when scores of branch lines were closed wholesale, and minor mainline stations shut. Many of their associated pubs survived, however, unless too far isolated from the village the station purported to serve – not an uncommon feature of many branch lines – with names including 'railway', 'station' and 'locomotive' being obvious clues to their former status. Others remain where the railway is still, like the pub, very much a part of everyday life.

THE CANAL PUBS

Ignoring failed or abandoned schemes and short spurs, within the county of Worcestershire there are, or have been, sections of two major canals plus a pair of shorter, minor ones. The principal two, coming in from the north, are the Staffordshire & Worcestershire Canal linking Wolverhampton with the River Severn at Stourport-on-Severn and, a few miles to the east, the Worcester & Birmingham

The Black Star, Stourport-on-Severn, one of the county's several excellent canalside pubs.

Canal linking Birmingham with the River Severn further downstream at Worcester. In this new age of leisure use, both these canals are popular with narrowboat users from the Midlands, and are often used in conjunction with the stretch of the Severn between Stourport and Worcester, and the revitalised Birmingham Canal Navigations, to make for a long circular trip through some delightfully varied – and historically important – surroundings.

At one time a third canal link to the Severn was provided by the Droitwich Junction Canal, which left the Worcester & Birmingham at Hanbury Wharf to flow westwards to Droitwich, where it met the Droitwich Canal, which then continued on to join the river at Hawford, north of Worcester. Today both sections of this waterway are virtually derelict, though short stretches have been reclaimed, notably at the eastern end, and there are ongoing attempts to re-open the entire length. Sadly, the Eagle & Sun at Hanbury Wharf, a lovely little traditional canal pub has, in recent times, been turned into an up-market eatery with the redevelopment of that end of the Droitwich Junction Canal as moorings.

The canal pubs described here are listed in a north to south order, with those of the Staffordshire & Worcestershire first, then the Worcester & Birmingham.

Staffordshire & Worcestershire Canal

CAUNSALL: ANCHOR INN

Caunsall Road, Caunsall, Kidderminster, DY11 5YL · 01562 850254 · www.theanchorinncaunsall.co.uk

Turn left off the A449 Wolverhampton Road from Kidderminster after the two turn-offs for Cookley

The Staffordshire & Worcestershire Canal, engineered by the famous canal builder James Brindley between 1766 and 1772, runs for just over 46 miles from Great Haywood on the Trent & Mersey Canal via Wolverhampton and Kidderminster to Stourport-on-Severn, then merely a hamlet by the name of Lower Mitton. It had been planned for the canal to join the Severn at Bewdley but the town's elders refused to have the terminus of the 'stinking ditch' there! Widely regarded as one of the prettiest canals in England, it enters Worcestershire a little above Caunsall, where the first of the canalside pubs in the county is to be found.

Although not sited directly beside the canal towpath, the Anchor Inn on the corner of Caunsall Road and New Road west off the A451 – as its sign acknowledges – is most definitely a canal pub for it was licensed in 1840, as part of an existing

The Anchor Inn, Caunsall.

The Anchor's link to the canal: follow the path across the meadow to the bridge over the Stour.

farmworker's cottage, to serve the boats that passed along this winding stretch of the canal just a few yards away. The first landlord, farmworker William Taylor, did not brew his own beer but was supplied by Frederick Mills of Rose Cottage nearby (who also supplied a number of other local pubs).

The Anchor remained a free house until 1945 when it was sold to Twist's White Horse Brewery in Walsall; five years later this brewery was taken over by Atkinson's Brewery of Aston in Birmingham, itself taken over in 1959 by one of the two West Midlands giants, Mitchells & Butlers of Smethwick. Today though it is once again a free house, Pete Green, the current landlord, having bought it back into the family in 1991. It is extremely popular with locals and those who make the journey especially to sample its excellent beer, cider and cobs; on any given day the clientele might well range from a visiting group of motorbikers to the local MP.

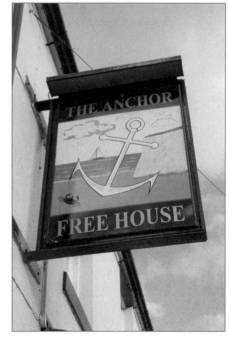

Pete Green's grandfather, Ralph Barker, took over the pub in 1927, buying it outright for £1,800 nine years later; the existing furniture dates back to the 1920s. Inside there is a small snug and a larger main bar room, the latter once being half the present size but knocked through to a private living room behind (the remains of the fireplace there are clearly visible). The horse racing memorabilia decorating the walls reflect the interest of the current landlord, and for many years the local hunt met here before setting off. A very attractive but unrelated period feature, in full view of anyone

The public bar.

sitting in one of the two bay windows, is the Victorian postbox set into the old brick wall opposite; this is complemented by a traditional red telephone kiosk beside the pub, all adding to the charm of the scene.

The pub is also close to the River Stour – a decorative iron bridge across it links the pub with the canal – but cannot be regarded as a mug house since the Stour above Kidderminster, apart from a very brief period in the 1660s, was never a commercial waterway, or indeed suitable for upgrading to that status – hence the construction of the canal alongside it a hundred years later.

WOLVERLEY: LOCK INN

Wolverley Road, Wolverley, DY10 3RN · 01562 850581

By the canal bridge and lock on the B4189 Wolverley Road, midway between the A442 and the A449 immediately north of Kidderminster

After leaving Caunsall the Staffordshire & Worcestershire continues to run parallel with the River Stour – which is little more than a stream here – passing under part of the village of Cookley in a short tunnel before winding its way through a delightful, wooded landscape to the east and south of the small, picturesque village of Wolverley. The buildings here occupy the higher ground beyond the meadows of the river's floodplain where the smaller Horsebrook joins the

The Lock Inn, Wolverley, as near to the canal lock as it is possible for a pub to be.

The great fireplace . . .

. . . and the public bar
counter.

Stour. Immediately before the canal passes under the Wolverley road is a lock, beside which is sited the Lock Inn, on the corner of Lea Lane.

The village takes its name from a Saxon chieftain by the name of Wulfweard, who in 886 was given the land here by the then King of Mercia, Burgred – hence the name 'Wulfweard's open land'. Since then the settlement has flourished, the

The view from the upstairs room,
across the canal and the Stour
towards the parish church.

principal industry in more recent times (other than agriculture) being iron working.
A feature of the village is a number of habitations carved out of the red sandstone
outcrops in the village, used by iron workers during the Industrial Revolution – and
in some cases inhabited until well after the Second World War. Such dwellings are
not uncommon in this region, the most famous being at Kinver Edge just over the
West Midlands boundary to the north.

The Lock Inn is a homely, unpretentious pub dating from just after the
construction of the canal, comprising a main public bar, complete with a large open
fire, and second room downstairs, plus an upstairs dining room. A small terraced
area beside the pub is as close to the canal as it can be and affords customers an
excellent viewpoint from which to watch the workings of the lock. Kidderminster is a
little more than a mile along the towpath to the south while at the same distance to
the north, either along the towpath or the quiet Lea Lane beside it, is the Eagle &
Spur at Cookley (see Chapter 4) and half a mile beyond that, the Anchor at Caunsall,
making possible a very pleasant and very manageable circular mini pub crawl.

The name of Charles II crops up in connection with this pub for, although the
Lock Inn dates from after his time, he crossed the Stour at this point in 1651, on his
way to exile, after fleeing from the Battle of Worcester.

STOURPORT-ON-SEVERN: *BIRD IN HAND*

Holly Road, Stourport-on-Severn, DY13 9BA · 01299 822385

Approaching the town from Kidderminster on the A451 (Minster Road), follow the one-way system left into Gilgal, then first left into Baldwin Road, first left into Holly Road. From the A4025 Worcester Road, turn left at the Hartlebury Road island, then first right into Baldwin Road

Entering the north-eastern outskirts of Stourport, the first pub reached on the Staffordshire & Worcestershire is the Bird in Hand, at what was once a busy spot on the canal with its own wharf for the local farms and mills, and a 'winding hole' on the opposite bank to enable boats to be turned around. Traces of this can still be seen. On the other side of the canal the wooded ground rises steeply to St Michael's churchyard, said to be the largest in England.

Approaching the Bird in Hand, Stourport-on-Severn, from the canal towpath.

The Bird in Hand's stunning canalside aspect.

The pub, now encroached upon by modern housing, possibly predates the building of the canal in 1771; certainly by the 1820s it had became an important canal pub for watermen, waggoners and locals from the neighbouring cottages. One notable licensee, from 1901 to 1943, was Benjamin Evers, a musician who with his five sons founded the Stourport Town Band in 1901 (and which continued to practise in a designated band room upstairs until 1966). His daughter played the piano for showings of silent movies in the town.

In 1964 a major refurbishment was carried out, with one of the two downstairs bar rooms being enlarged and a dining area added with the conversion of the former stable block, though this was tastefully executed without the loss of too much

The roadside frontage of the Bird in Hand.

The Bird in Hand's sign: a
modern twist on an old image.

atmosphere. Good food is very much a feature of the pub, which is justifiably popular
with canal and towpath users, and locals wishing to enjoy a drink or a meal away
from the bustle of the town centre.

The pub's name – a fairly common one in England – is thought to derive from the
saying 'A bird in the hand is worth two in the bush', and the sign is traditionally
illustrated with a falcon perched on a mailed fist.

STOUPORT-ON-SEVERN: *BLACK STAR*

1 Mitton Street, Stourport-on-Severn, DY13 8YP · 01299 822404

At the junction of Mitton Street and Lion Hill at the top of the High Street.
No parking but public car parks are within a few minutes' walk

Shortly before joining the River Severn at the large and historically fascinating locks and basins complex in Stourport, the Staffordshire & Worcestershire passes under two road bridges in the centre of the town. Beside the first of these, carrying Mitton Street, is the Black Star pub overlooking the canal towpath. Upper and Lower Mitton were the names for the area before it was renamed Stourport with the coming of the canal.

The pub is first recorded as early as 1780 as the Star, though it is very possible that before that it was known as the Star & Hammer, the licensee being John Bates. As is readily apparent when viewed side-on, the present-day establishment is made up of three different buildings, now knocked-through. The one nearest the road is the original pub behind which was the much larger Mitton House, possibly once a chapel. This carries a plaque dated 1884

The canal frontage of the Black Star, Stourport-on-Severn, by the road bridge, showing clearly the two very different buildings added behind the original pub.

In the cosy public bar of the Black Star.

bearing that name and the intitials of Eli Hitchon, licensee from 1876 to 1887; behind this building the end, smaller structure bears a smaller plaque with the initials 'E.H.' and '1883', both dates presumably recording the years the buildings were erected. This end portion of the pub is thought to have been built as a school for the children of the canal boat families; it had separate entrances for boys and girls.

The Black Star also served as a coaching inn during the first part of the nineteenth century, with services to Wolverhampton and Worcester, but by 1835 only the Worcester to Bewdley coach called there. No longer reliant on the canal for its trade, the pub is a thriving local with the original portion retained as a traditional bar, backed by a dining area with its own bar, and a toilet and kitchen block. Music nights are held on Tuesdays and Saturdays.

The use of 'star' as a pub's name dates back to the fifteenth century and is almost certainly another one of religious derivation, in this case comemmorating the Star of Bethlehem. The addition of 'hammer' is unusual and possibly a tribute to the local foundry workers. It is thought that 'black' was added to the pub's name with the cutting of the canal, as a reference to the black star formed by the rose of a maritime compass.

Worcester & Birmingham Canal

ALVECHURCH: *WEIGHBRIDGE*

Scarfield Wharf, Scarfield Hill, Alvechurch, B48 7SQ · 0121 445 5111 · www.the-weighbridge.co.uk

Part of the Alvechurch marina on the west bank of the Worcester & Birmingham Canal, on the continuation of Bar Hill and Station Road from the centre of Alvechurch. Five minutes' walk from Alvechurch railway station

The 30-mile Worcester & Birmingham Canal, begun in the 1790s but not fully opened until 1815, enters Worcestershire by way of the 1½-mile West Hill tunnel from King's Norton in south Birmingham, emerging near Hopwood in the north-east corner of the county.

The Weighbridge is one of Worcestershire's youngest pubs, though the red-brick building is late eighteenth-century in age. In its former life it was the weighbridge office handling the offloading of coal, for local delivery, from canal barges to horses and carts, in the days when virtually every house or commercial premises demanded a constant supply of the fuel. With the dwindling of commercial traffic on the canals in the twentieth century, the office was closed in the 1920s and converted into two private residences; these later became one larger residence. With the resurgence in canal traffic from the 1960s onwards – this time in the form of leisure boats – the house became a cruising club before its latest transformation in 2002.

Inside the pub – which is owned by the marina – are a small public bar, a snug and a dining area, while outside is a large patio and beer garden. Beer from the independent breweries of the region is a speciality, as is the home-cooked food – both of which have helped the Weighbridge win several CAMRA awards during its short life. Themed food evenings are a regular event, and beer festivals are held twice a year. During the cruising season breakfast is also served, if booked in advance.

Worcestershire's youngest canalside pub, opened in 2002: the Weighbridge at Alvechurch.

In the public bar, with the serving hatch for the snug in the wall on the left.

Alvechurch was once a thriving little village in a delightful rural setting in the north-east of the county, but since the opening of the A441 immediately to the east, and the M42 to the north, it has been enlarged by much residential development to become a dormitory village for Birmingham; the old heart still remains, though.

STOKE PRIOR: *BOAT & RAILWAY INN*

Shaw Lane, Stoke Prior, B60 4EQ · 01527 831065

Located west off the B4091 Hanbury Road, accessed via either Shaw Lane to the north of the canal or Westonhall Road to the south. Parking on the road

Beyond Alvechurch, the Worcester & Birmingham Canal alters course slightly to run in a generally south-westerly direction towards Bromsgrove, passing to the east and south of the town; there are no canalside pubs along this rural, heavily-locked stretch at all. Immediately to the south of Bromsgrove though, in a more industrial and residential area known as Stoke Prior, the pubs reappear. Of these, one of the most traditional is the Boat & Railway Inn on the west bank of the canal at the junction of Shaw Lane and Westonhall Road, just south of where the latter road crosses over the Worcester & Birmingham Canal.

The Boat & Railway is an attractive, mid-Victorian red-brick building sandwiched tightly between the road and the waterway. Inside, it comprises a long public bar room sub-divided into two different areas (which would have once been separate rooms), both furnished in a traditional late-Victorian/Edwardian style with the decor in one slightly more basic than in the other. Both have open fires. There is a separate carvery and restaurant at one end of the pub together with a large, private function room – a recent conversion of a skittle alley. Outside at the back of the main building is a narrow, partially covered canalside terrace.

The Boat & Railway Inn, Stoke Prior.

The Boat & Railway's attractive canalside aspect.

Confusingly, the Boat & Railway is sometimes described as being situated in Stoke Works, with this name appearing on some maps and road signs. Stoke Prior is the

The door onto the canal terrace, with the pub's sign above to inform and entice passing boaters.

name for this whole region to the south of Bromsgrove, with its isolated farms and small groups of houses, while Stoke Works is the name given to one such group of houses around the pub. These dwellings were built primarily as houses for the workers employed at a huge local salt extraction plant, the works giving its name to the settlement. The plant was developed in the 1850s and 1860s by John Corbett, an engineer who devised the principle of pumping water into the underground seams of salt so that brine could be pumped out and the salt extracted, a far more efficient method of operation than traditional mining. Like several other Victorian industrialists, he was given to philanthropic gestures, in his case including the building of a small estate of terraced houses – many now replaced by more modern ones – for his employees.

The 'Railway' part of the pub's name is also connected with the salt works. In 1840

The lounge end of the bar area and the bar counter . . .

. . . and fireplace, with the raised Banks's logo on the metal fire surround – an unobtrusive period feature once found in many of the company's pubs.

the Birmingham & Gloucester Railway opened, linking the two cities and passing close to the west bank of the canal. A station was opened, but this closed to passengers in 1855. A second one, opened on a short linking line from here to Droitwich, opened in 1852 and closed in 1966. Gone too, is the goods branch that once connected the main line with the works' own railway system – just as the railway superseded the canal, so the lorry has largely displaced the railway as regards the carriage of goods.

WORCESTER: *ANCHOR INN*

54 Diglis Road, Worcester, WR5 3BW · 01905 351094

*Off the A38 Commandery Road/Bath Road south of the city centre.
There is limited parking on the opposite side of the road*

The very last pub on the Worcester & Birmingham is sited by the large basin at Diglis Locks where the canal enters the Severn. Fairly small and unassuming in appearance (as indeed are the majority of canalside pubs), it dates from the cutting of the canal but was remodelled in the middle of the nineteenth century, as is evident by the change of angle and style of the frontage compared with the adjoining cottage. Very much a canal-orientated establishment, a full English breakfast is available from 10 a.m. onwards for hungry boaters (and takeaways from 9 a.m.)

Diglis is a district to the south of the city centre, by the Severn, and during the eighteenth century it was developed as a recreational area outside the confines of the city. Here could be found assembly rooms (for cards, dances and the like), a riding school, a bowling green and even a cockpit. By the mid-nineteenth century though, these activities had been abandoned as a result of changing social behaviour, pressure for housing and other development – and a fatal stabbing.

It is currently home to a major redevelopment centred on the canal basin here, onto which the Anchor backs. The basin was built in the 1890s for the

Where the Worcester & Birmingham Canal meets the River Severn. The Anchor Inn, Worcester, beneath its current coating of dust from all the building work going on around it.

The entrance to the Anchor's beer garden, with the redevelopment of the Diglis canal basin well underway.

The welcoming entrance hallway, with the public bar off to the left and the snug off to the right.

transshipping of goods between canal barges and sea-going vessels, but never saw the volume of traffic for which it was designed except during the Second World War; today it is very much a leisure craft marina. Interestingly though, the Anchor's licensee in 1902 was a Mrs Hannah Mason whose secondary occupation was a coal merchant, presumably selling on coal brought in by barge or boat from elsewhere. Back towards the city centre, many of the semi-derelict canalside buildings have been converted into apartments, and blocks of new ones built on cleared industrial sites, with the whole area fast becoming a desirable residential district as a consequence.

The welcoming public and upper bars at the Anchor Inn.

Entrance to the Anchor – Worcester CAMRA's 2006 Pub of the Year – is via a short entrance hallway, off which is a small snug and a slightly larger public bar, off which in turn are a small lower-level seating and darts area, and a higher-level lounge with its own little bar doubling as a private function room. A curious feature is the skewed alignment of the old floor tiles in the main room – possibly a legacy from when the pub was remodelled. Many other original features remain, embellished by canal boat-style decorative touches. Outside there is a beer garden at the rear, and a skittle alley.

At the time of writing the future of this Marston's pub is slightly uncertain in that, given the redevelopment going on around it, the danger is that it will be given one of the brewery's bland makeovers, so destroying much of its existing character.

THE RAILWAY PUBS

In terms of the number of routes drawn upon it, the railway map of Worcestershire is far more crowded than that showing the canals. The railway history of the county is a long and complicated one, with a myriad of promoting companies eventually joining forces by 1923 as the two principal players in the region, the Midland Railway and Great Western Railway. Taking Worcester as the focus of the network, main lines ran north to Birmingham via Droitwich Spa and Kidderminster, and Droitwich Spa and Bromsgrove; east via Pershore to Evesham (and thence London); south to Cheltenham (and thence Gloucester and South Wales), and south-west via Great Malvern to Hereford (and thence North Wales).

The railway pubs described here are listed in date order of the opening of the lines they served.

KIDDERMINSTER: *RAILWAY BELL HOTEL*

Comberton Hill, Kidderminster, DY10 1QN · 01562 515680

On the A448 Kiddeminster to Bromsgrove road, opposite the approach to the railway stations

The major carpet-weaving town of Kidderminster was joined to the growing national railway network in 1852 when, on 1 May that year, the grandly entitled Oxford, Worcester & Wolverhampton Railway – known to its detractors as 'the Old Worse & Worse' – opened the station there on its line linking the places of its title via Evesham, Kidderminster and Dudley. Ten years later a second concern, the Severn Valley Railway, opened its line from Hartlebury, south of Kidderminster, to Bewdley, a little to the west, on 1 February 1862 (and thence on to Shrewsbury); ten years later again, both the OWW and the SVR were absorbed by the Great Western Railway. To complete the picture, on 1 June 1878 the GWR opened a linking line between Kidderminster and Bewdley.

Today the main line from Worcester is still open through Kidderminster, only now running to Birmingham rather than Wolverhampton, with the station served by no less than three pubs within a 100-yard radius – and there was until recently a fourth just a few yards further on!

The Railway Bell Hotel, Kidderminster.

The Railway Bell as it looked in Edwardian times, on a postcard sent in 1908 from just round the corner. Note the (short-lived) tramway connecting the station with the town centre. (*Author's collection*)

The pub's sign was repainted in the 1990s and depicts an express locomotive in blue livery rather than the more appropriate Great Western green.

The red-brick Railway Bell Hotel, opened in 1855, is located immediately opposite the turn-in for Kidderminster station – Station Approach – and, as its name suggests, once offered accommodation for railway travellers in the manner of its innumerable counterparts up and down the country. Also conforming to type in its architecture and layout, it boasts one large, basically furnished public bar (with a real fire) and a smaller, barless back room on the ground floor; there is a small side terrace overlooking the road, popular on hot days. A large, private function room occupies the first floor, and is still used for club meetings, talks, and music performances – local rock luminaries Robert Plant, Stan Webb and Mike Sanchez have all performed here.

The pub has been altered very little over the last century and a half – apart from the usual improvements to the toilets – though signs of the times are reflected in the several

Afternoon dominoes in the Railway Bell. Looking on is landlord Bill Campbell.

Happy faces behind the bar.

prominent TV screens, for as well as refreshing railway travellers the pub also serves as a local for the streets of terraced houses behind it, and is extremely popular with football fans (Kidderminster Harriers' football ground is just a short distance away) as well as anyone wishing to watch the horse racing, rugby, cricket or snooker during the afternoon and evening. Sporting activity is not always external: the traditional pub games of darts, cribbage and dominoes are also popular here. Be warned – it can get extremely crowded on local, and international, match days.

Food is not served, though when you are right next door to the national award-winning Captain Cod's Fish Bar, that is not a problem.

KIDDERMINSTER: *KING & CASTLE*

Station Approach, Kidderminster, DY10 1QN · 01562 747505

Off the A448 Kidderminster to Bromsgrove road next to the main line railway station

The second of Kidderminster's railway pubs described here may appear to be an odd choice for inclusion in a book on historic pubs, considering that it is little more than twenty years old. It is here though because, despite its age, it is a genuine railway pub of a traditional kind: one incorporated into the very structure of a station. Its pre-history began in the 1960s when the former Severn Valley Railway, together with its Bewdley–Kidderminster connection, was closed by British Railways in stages, the last two sections used by passenger trains to go (in January 1970) being those between Bewdley and Hartlebury, and Bewdley and Kidderminster; the very last section of just a few hundred yards, used by goods trains serving the sugar beet factory in Kidderminster, was closed ten years later. In 1965 though, the Severn Valley Railway Society was set up to preserve as much of the line as possible and since then the railway has been reopened in stages from Bridgnorth south to Kidderminster, the southern terminus being opened on 30 July 1984 to complete what had become one of Britain's premier steam railways.

The Kidderminster station building – opposite the Railway Bell and just a few yards from the main line station – was built on the site of the former goods yard beside the main line station. It was based on a traditional GWR design as prepared for a new station at Ross-on-Wye in Herefordshire, a fact commemorated in an inscribed stone set into the back wall:

The main entrance to the King & Castle, Kidderminster, allowing access even when the station is shut.

KIDDERMINSTER TOWN STATION
SEVERN VALLEY RAILWAY
BASED UPON A DESIGN PREPARED FOR ROSS-ON-WYE STATION
ORIGINALLY PREPARED IN 1890 BY J.E. DANKS OF
THE G.W.R. CIVIL ENGINEER'S DEPT. PADDINGTON

The back door to the King & Castle, and the windows from which patrons can watch the steam trains arriving and departing.

The contractor for the construction was the Black Country firm of William Jackson (Langley Green) Ltd. Built in red and dark blue brick, the new station building was to comprise a central frontage block with two wings behind leading towards the platforms; in the event half of the east wing was not completed, and a temporary cafeteria substituted. The west wing was opened on 24 November 1984 and the central block, one half of which was given over to the King & Castle, on 28 September of the following year. The official opening, by Michael Spicer MP, the Parliamentary Under Secretary of State for Transport, was on 4 July 1986. Completion of the east wing to house an eighty-seater Refreshment Room (which, as the Valley Suite, doubles as a function room), and the installation of a glass canopy over the space between the two wings, came when, on 18 October 2006, the SVR's patron, the Duke of Gloucester, formally declared it open.

The King & Castle, though physically part of the station, is a pub in its own right and is open even if the station is not. In layout it is very much of the time of its 1890 design: immediately beyond the doorway is a bar counter and a tiled floor area for standing customers, with a carpeted lounge area beyond that. Notable features include the specially commissioned replica carpet with its GWR motif, the large real fire at the end of the lounge, a display of railwayana (including working clocks) on the walls, and the bar counter's marble top and wooden fittings salvaged from the old refreshment room at Worcester Foregate Street station. The pub has featured

The single bar room, finished in authentic Great Western colours and sporting a specially commissioned replica carpet.

Head barman John, in typical jovial mood.

frequently in CAMRA's *Good Beer Guide* over the years and can boast its own, specially brewed (and exceedingly cheap) bitter: Royal Piddle, from the Wyre Piddle Brewery.

Visitors should note that since the Refreshment Room opened, food is no longer served in the King & Castle – whose name, incidentally, derives only indirectly from kings and castles in the conventional sense, glorifying as it does the GWR's King and Castle classes, Swindon-built express passenger locomotives from the golden age of steam. The pub is very popular with visitors to the railway and local residents alike, with the former often delighted to find that, at the other end of the line, the original station building at Bridgnorth incorporates the Railwayman's Arms, the SVR's other pub (and equally worthy of a visit).

RIPPLE: *RAILWAY INN*

Station Road, Ripple, Tewkesbury, GL20 6EY · 01684 592225

First left off the A38 Tewkesbury to Worcester road coming north from Junction 1 on the M50, then continue on through the village as far as the old railway bridge

Despite its postcode, the village of Ripple is most definitely in Worcestershire – but only just, located right on the Gloucestershire border some three miles north of Tewkesbury. It is an unspoilt little village – still with its stocks and whipping post – which almost certainly takes its name from the Old English rippel, meaning a tongue of land, in this case that formed by the converging rivers Severn and Avon. Its Civil War claim to fame is that it was here that the Royalists won their last victory before being defeated at the 1651 Battle of Worcester, foiling the Parliamentarians' plan to march on Upton and destroy the bridge there.

The Railway Inn, Ripple.

A skittles match in progress in the purpose-built indoor alley.
This ancient pub game remains in a very healthy state in the
southern half of the county, the Worcestershire variant being
just one of a whole family of traditional games based on
bowling or throwing balls or batons at standing objects.

The Railway Inn's sign, inappropriately depicting the Great
Western Railway's coat of arms in its 1903 version
incorporating the shields and mottoes of the cities of London
and Bristol. The branch and station belonged to the GWR's
arch-rival, the Midland Railway!

For nearly a century Ripple was served by the Midland Railway's branch line
connecting Great Malvern with Tewkesbury via Upton-upon-Severn. The station
opened with the railway in 1864 and closed, with the surviving Upton to
Tewkesbury portion of the line, in 1961. It has now been converted into a private
house. In many rural localities, the railway passed some distance from the village it
purported to serve – a direct route taking precedence over the villagers' convenience
– but Ripple was an exception to the rule with the line running through its centre.

The Railway Inn, opened with the railway, stands by the bridge carrying Station
Road over the former railway cutting, almost opposite the approach to the old station
yard and building. It is a homely, unpretentious pub that is a genuine village local –
helped by its status as the only one in the village – sub-divided into a number of small
areas for drinking and dining, plus a small outside seating area at the front. As a
genuine local it is host to a whole range of activities, some making use of the spacious
skittle alley at the rear. Besides its importance to the local community, the Railway
Inn is one of the very few relatively unspoilt railway pubs left in Worcestershire.

FOUR

Locals

Call frequently,
Drink moderately,
Pay honourably,
Be good company,
Part friendly,
Go home quietly.

From the Claines Mug House leaflet op. cit.

While it could be said that the pubs in this chapter have been included because they do not fall into any of the other categories, that would not be the full story. The village or town 'local' provides a very special service in its own right: that of providing a social focus for its immediate surroundings and community. Often hidden away in back streets, housing estates and rural byways, they are usually relatively small and unpretentious – but they are no less important than any other type of pub. Indeed, they can claim the honour of representing the oldest type of pub for the concept of the local is as old as that of the pub itself. It is in these pubs that the county's darts and skittle leagues flourish, where football and cricket teams are based, where rafts are built for the annual races on the Severn and quizzes are held, where local societies meet and where village affairs are organised.

One type of local though was often rather more grand: the market tavern. For almost as long as man has traded and bartered, there have been organised and designated marketplaces; for almost as long as there have been marketplaces there have been market taverns – often in the plural – overlooking them. Here, in warmth and comfort after a hard day's bargaining, deals would be sealed over a pint or two, news and gossip caught up with, old acquaintances resumed and a hearty meal partaken of before the long trudge home. For those customers from further afield – merchants, commercial travellers and the like – accommodation was also to be had.

Marketplaces still flourish today, though the more specialised ones such as local cattle markets have tended to move out of town, merge with another, or disappear entirely. For their part however, the old market taverns have tended to survive as locals on non-market days though, as with all categories of pubs, some have closed and others have changed their names. Sadly, few of the county's surviving examples

At the heart of any good local is the public bar. This is the one at the Bell & Cross in Clent; in the back wall is a tiny serving hatch for villagers wanting to buy drinks to take away without being seen by anybody in the pub.

are in anything like their original condition. Even when the market is no longer there, the name of a pub can be a very good indication of what was once close by. To take but one Worcestershire example: in Kidderminster there are, or have been, pubs called the Corn Exchange, the Market Hall Vaults, the Market Tavern and the Farmer's Boy situated by the various indoor, outdoor and cattle markets.

Sadly, the number of locals still in business has declined dramatically in recent years right across Britain, with Worcestershire no exception. The reasons for this decline are many, but central to them all is the fact that the brewers and pub chains who own many of them would rather sell or redevelop them as residential or other commercial properties than be content with their takings, scant as they often are in relation to far bigger, main-road eateries with their higher profit margins on food, and brash, town centre, youth-orientated bars with their emphasis on 'vertical drinking' whereby customers are encouraged to stand more or less upright, gawp at TV screens and drink as much as possible.

Thankfully, the decline appears to be slowing – in rural areas at least – with local authorities increasingly reluctant to approve any change of use for such premises, especially if it would mean the loss of a village's only pub. Such an attitude is only to be applauded. Also, the sheer weight of numbers will ensure that many of Worcestershire's locals will undoubtedly survive, especially those in or near areas of high-density housing. Those included here are listed in alphabetical order of place.

ABBERLEY: *MANOR ARMS*

Netherton Lane, Abberley Village, WR6 6BN · 01299 896507 ·
www.themanorarms.co.uk

Coming on the A443 Worcester to Newnham Bridge Road, turn right after
Great Witley onto the B4202, then first or second right to the village

Located on the Abberley Hills roughly equidistant from Kidderminster to the
north-east and Worcester to the south-east, the older part of the village of
Abberley is home to the partially ruined Norman church of St Michael with, as
is so often the case, the village pub directly opposite. Old Abberley is a relatively
unspoilt and charming little cluster of buildings, well off the beaten track at a
convergence of winding country lanes in a hilly and wooded north-western part of
the county (but on the Worcestershire Way long-distance footpath, which passes the
Manor Arms' front door). The more modern part of the village is some half a mile to
the west, on the B4202 Clows Top Lane. The name of the village derives from
'Ealdbeald's clearing' (leah).

The pub is believed to date back to the end of the seventeenth century and was
originally part of the estate of the local Lord of the Manor – hence its name – and
was once used as a courthouse; a tunnel, now bricked-up, led to a small gaol
opposite. The manorial link is commemorated further with an imposing display of
the coats of arms of the former lords on the building's façade.

The Manor Arms, Abberley.

The lounge bar counter, with landlord Jason Seldon on the left.

The magnificent lounge bar fireplace.

There are two principal rooms; a public bar, named the Owen Glyndwr Bar after the Welsh leader who was hunted by Henry IV through the surrounding countryside, and a lounge bar with a magnificent inglenook fireplace beyond which is a small secluded dining area known as the Alcoves; this is the oldest portion of the building and was once part of the pub's private living quarters. (The large dressed stones forming the fireplace are thought to have come from the ruins of a local castle.) A restaurant/function room and patio at the rear of the pub command delightful views over the rolling countryside to the north, with catering ranging from bar snacks to full meals, pre-booked parties and wedding receptions. A marquee is also available. A recent change of landlord has seen a revival in the pub's fortunes after a period of neglect. Emphasis is placed on events such as regular themed food nights with special occasions throughout the year, such as Burns' Night and St George's Day, being marked in appropriate fashion. Accommodation is also provided.

An unmissable feature at the front of the pub is the height of the entrance above the roadway – probably deliberately built that way to allow for easy mounting and dismounting of horses. (Elsewhere, strategically-placed stone blocks have been provided outside important buildings for the same purpose.) It also ensures that rainwater running down the road outside cannot enter the building.

BEWDLEY: *LITTLE PACK HORSE*

32 High Street, Bewdley, DY12 2PH · 01299 403762

*Coming west from the Severn bridge (B4190), turn left at the top of
Load Street into the High Street. No parking – use one of the public car parks
in the town*

Known as the Pack Horse before 1982, this tiny pub is well-hidden in its very
misleadingly named road: a narrow, residential thoroughfare that is less like a
High Street than probably any other in the county. Entrance to the pub's one
bar room is via a covered side alley; immediately off the bar is a smaller, secluded
dining area with an extensive menu. Exposed beams and timbers, a log stove, bare
floorboards and tiles all add to the intimate atmosphere. The pub's name indicates
that it was originally a carriers' pub, providing accommodation and stabling for
horses.

The Pack Horse's first recorded licensee was James Lane in 1818, though the
building is certainly much older than that. It was certainly trading in 1808 as one of
seven alehouses in the town, which fact led it later to advertise itself as 'The Oldest

The Little Pack Horse, Bewdley, hidden away from the main tourist areas in the town.

The Pack Horse's single bar.

Established House For Refreshments in this Ancient Borough'. It was certainly a popular pub for in 1895 a friendly society known as the Bewdley Working Men's Sick & Dividend Society (whose motto was 'Help one another to bear each other's burden') was formed there, and it was also the headquarters of the Bewdley & District Terrier Club and the Bewdley Homing Society.

The Pack Horse was one of the last brew pubs in the town, with beer production ceasing as late as 1940. Four years later it was sold to the Holt Brewery Co. of Birmingham (which, ten years earlier, had become part of the Ansell & Sons group of companies). It became a quiet, back-street pub until it was purchased in 1982 by the legendary Colm 'Mad' O'Rourke, an entrepreneur who specialised in buying run-down pubs and refurbishing them in a unique way, eventually establishing a much-loved empire of 'Little Pubs' across the West Midlands. In his pubs one could sit at old butchers' blocks or other strange-looking tables, dine on a giant 'Desperate Dan Cow Pie' washed down with a pint or two of the pubs' own bitter (Lumphammer), all the while surrounded by a glorious profusion of old machines of indefinable purpose, great murals of home-produced tiles, displays of old tools and advertising material, and racks and rows of mugs and other ornaments decorated with the pubs' names and signs. There were pub trails to be completed, games to be played and comic newspapers to be read – and with each pub retaining its own special indentity. One even had a large chunk of a canal narrowboat serving as a bar and another an old trawler parked on its front lawn!

In 1998 the Little Pubs were sold, the Little Pack Horse being one of those bought by Ushers of Trowbridge, since reborn as the InnSpired pubco. It still, happily, retains some decorative items dating from the O'Rourke era.

Bewdley: *Woodcolliers Arms*

76 Welch Gate, Bewdley, DY12 2HU · 01299 400589

*Coming west from the Severn bridge (B4190), turn right at the top of
Load Street then left at the junction into Welch Gate. Two parking spaces
(but reserved spaces for guests), or use one of the public car parks in the town*

This long, L-shaped pub stands in Welch Gate – 'the street leading to Wales' – at the corner of Winbrook and Sandy Bank (and on National Cycle Route 45 from Salisbury to Chester). Externally it is obvious that it has been enlarged over the years with incorporation of neighbouring buildings; internally the succession of partitioned-off areas on different levels – including two bar counters – confirm that it was once five separate buildings (with a passageway between two of them), one of which was a cottage, one a cobbler's shop and another – that fronting Welch Gate – the Squirrel public house. (This part of the town was once thick with pubs now long gone.) At one time there was also a smoke room upstairs. Thankfully, no attempt has been made to turn the building into a one-room, one-bar establishment and a multitude of original features survive in what is now a Grade II listed building.

The Woodcolliers Arms, Bewdley. The right-hand end of the building was remodelled slightly when the main road was widened.

The higher-level bar: the counter and the connecting door to the rest of the pub . . .

. . . and the far, fireplace end. This part of the room was once in a separate building, across an alleyway from the area shown in the previous photograph.

It is thought that before the 1871 Census, the pub – or its direct predecessor – was named the Black Boy, and possibly dates to 1808 or before. It then appears in a 1836 trade directory as the Wood Colliers. In the 1851 Census the licensee was given as George Cooke, a woodcollier by trade; in 1868 it was Joseph Cooke, another woodcollier, then in 1871 Eliza Cooke. The former publicans' other occupation had by then, however, given its name to the pub. A woodcollier (sometimes spelled as two words) was a charcoal burner: that is, someone who made charcoal by the slow burning or cooking of wood in very little oxygen in order to remove its moisture content. It was a traditional woodland trade, with great stacks of wood covered in turves and set alight to smoulder for days until ready. A plentiful supply of wood was to be had in the Wyre Forest immediately to the west of Bewdley, while the finished product had a wide variety of uses, especially in the forges of the small metal-smelting works and associated industries that once lined the River Severn here.

At the time of writing the pub is undergoing a sympathetic makeover after a change of licensee, with accommodation and authentic traditional Russian dishes now offered.

BEWDLEY: *BLACK BOY*

50 Wyre Hill, Bewdley, DY12 2UE · 01299 403523

Coming from Bewdley town centre, go left of the Woodcolliers Arms up Sandy Bank then Wyre Hill; coming from Tenbury Wells on the A456, go left into Long Bank at the Bewdley bypass roundabout, then bear right into Wyre Hill. No car park

A few hundred yards up the hill from the Woodcolliers Arms is the Black Boy, a cosy little three-room (public bar, lounge and snug or meeting room), two-level pub on what was once a main road out of Bewdley but which is now a quiet – but very steep – narrow lane lined with some delightful old buildings at the lower end. Inside can be found exposed beams and traditional padded wooden benches, and wood and iron pub tables. There is a beer garden to the rear of the pub with views over the old town and the Severn Valley.

The black-and-white half-timbered building dates back to at least the late sixteenth century, though it probably did not become an ale house until the following century; in 1820 the licensee was William Pountney. Pigot's 1835 trade directory lists it as having a brew house attached and beer was home-brewed on site

The Black Boy, Bewdley. The half of the pub on the right of the photograph is half-timbered, the half on the left merely has the 'beams' painted onto the brick wall! On the far right are cottages of the same period.

Regulars relaxing in the public bar, with the higher-level lounge just visible beyond the bar.

until the First World War or thereabouts. For most of the nineteenth century the licensee was a member of the Pountney family – other members ran other pubs in the Welch Gate area of the town – and the pub was run in conjunction with a small butcher's shop. In 1939 the pub was sold to Wolverhampton & Dudley Breweries. In more recent times the Black Boy has appeared regularly in listings of good pubs in the West Midlands region and is a popular calling-in place for beer lovers from Bewdley and further afield.

A warm welcome from Paul Willcox, husband of licensee Pat, behind the lounge bar . . .

. . . and with Fluffy 'Tiger' Willcox, one of the Black Boy's two cats.

The name of the pub derives from a nickname of Charles II, 'the black boy across the water' as the loyal toast had it at the time of his exile. His portrait is on the sign, complete with the swarthy features that gave rise to the nickname. The Black Boy was a name adopted by many pubs in both royalist and non-royalist areas to celebrate the restoration of the monarchy in 1660 – including, one suspects, by landlords with Cromwellian sympathies eager to hide them! Indeed, so popular was it that the name was also used at one time by the Woodcolliers Arms (p. 73) and by the Black Boy Hotel across the river in the district of Wribbenhall. (It should be noted that the depiction on the sign of pubs with this name of a negro boy or slave, or a sooty-faced chimney-sweep's boy, is almost always a later and erroneous alteration.)

BIRTSMORTON: *FARMERS ARMS*

Birts Street, Birtsmorton, WR13 6AP · 01684 833308

Take the B4208 north off the A438 Tewkesbury to Ledbury road, then turn right through Birts Street and bear left at the fork

Rural Worcestershire is home to some absolute gems of black-and-white half-timbered pubs, and the Farmers Arms in the south-west of the county is one of the best. Dating back to the fifteenth century, it is a long, two-storey building standing by a minor road junction in the scattered collection of hamlets

known as Birtsmorton a little to the south of the Malverns. The district's principal claim to fame is that it was the birthplace of William Huskisson, Member of Parliament for Liverpool and President of the Board of Trade, and the first man in the world to be killed by a passenger train, the occasion being the opening of the Liverpool & Manchester Railway in 1830.

Inside, the pub is almost completely unspoiled – and all the more special for that – and boasts one of the lowest ceiling beams you are ever likely to encounter. There is one long bar area, formed from two rooms at some time in the past, each with an open fire. It has long been popular with cycle clubs as a refreshment

The picturesque Farmers Arms, Birtsmorton.

The lounge bar, and below, the lounge and the beam that is not much more than 5ft off the floor!

The main entrance.

stop, no doubt partly because of its rural, flat location; it has also served as an archetypal 'olde English' backdrop for vehicle manufacturers (notably Land Rover) against which to photograph their products.

At the time of writing there is about to be a change of licensee, so exactly what the future might bring to the pub is slightly uncertain.

BRETFORTON: *FLEECE INN*

The Cross, Bretforton, WR11 7JE · 01386 831173 · www.thefleeceinn.co.uk

From Evesham, right off the B4305 Evesham to Banbury road in the heart of the village. Parking on the road

Choosing the one pub out of all those in this book that encapsulates all that is best in the pubs of Worcestershire would be an invidious task, but if pressed the authors would have to plump for the Fleece Inn in the Vale of Evesham. It is known locally as 'the Ark' after its previous name; the original name before that was the Blue Pump. Deservedly voted CAMRA's Worcestershire Pub of the Year in 2006, the Fleece has to be counted as one of the best half-dozen historic pubs in the whole of England.

Situated at one corner of The Cross, as the tiny village green in this charming south-west Worcestershire village is known, and dating in part from the fourteenth century, the main building of the Fleece was originally a stone-built longhouse (housing both people and animals) belonging to a farmer by the name of Byrd, and it remained in the hands of that family for several hundred years. It was first licensed on 28 May 1848 when, at the Excise Office at Evesham, a publican's licence was granted to Henry Byrd. A copy of the licence is on display in the inn.

The last private owner of the Fleece was Byrd's great-granddaughter, Miss Lola Taplin, who lived in the pub all her life and who, by all accounts, engendered a warm and welcoming atmosphere in the pub until she passed away peacefully in 1977, aged 83, in

The Fleece Inn, Bretforton.

front of the fire in the snug. Miss Taplin bequeathed the pub and its contents to the National Trust (and by so doing, made it the first pub to be owned by that body). This is not to say that she did not have her own idiosyncrasies. For example, an American who dared to ask for ice was told sharply that he would only get ice when it snowed, and anyone who dared to eat on the premises would be told to leave

In the garden, during the 2006 Asparagus Festival.

The courtyard: always popular on a summer's day.

forthwith! (This was a not uncommon trait of the old breed of publican, where a request for food would be met with the curt response, 'This is a bloody pub, not a restaurant'.) Legend maintains that Lola still keeps a watchful eye over goings-on – reincarnated as the owl perched on the roof ridge of the thatched barn beside the pub, and the builders employed to renovate the premises after her demise told tales of lunch boxes being overturned and their sandwiches being scattered. (The barn is a comparative youngster, dating as it does from the sixteenth century, and is used as an overflow room for the pub when special events are held. It can also be hired for private functions – and is now licensed for civil weddings.)

The inn made the news again in 2004, this time for all the wrong reasons. On 27 February that year a spark from the chimney set light to the thatched roof, resulting in the partial destruction of the original building; thanks to the fire service, complete disaster was averted. The Fleece has since been reconstructed (with a traditional stone-tiled roof) and the fittings, including a magnificent 300-year-old pewter display, restored. A new grapevine on the front, to replace the one that died shortly after Miss Taplin, now thrives. Inside, the idiosyncratic layout of panelled rooms, corridors and bar, with their stone-flagged floors and dark oak furniture, is as attractive as ever. Those familiar with the inn's most famous feature will be pleased to learn that the white 'witch circles' on the hearths, keeping witches from gaining access via the chimneys, have been repainted. (The cracks between the flagstones were also originally whitened to serve a similar purpose.) the building is Grade II listed and has a well-deserved place in CAMRA's National Inventory of Historic Pub Interiors.

Outside, the inn's courtyard, garden, orchard, barn and even The Cross play host to an all-year succession of special events, including classic car meets, fêtes, music nights – and a famous early summer Asparagus Festival and farmers' market. Dishes made from local ingredients are a speciality, and a double bedroom offers limited accommodation. A home catering service – including a whole pig roast – is also available.

The pub name commemorates the area's former importance and wealth as a wool-producing region (and can be encountered elsewhere in England for the same reason).

BROADWAY: *HORSE & HOUND*

54 High Street, Broadway, WR12 7DT · 01386 852287 ·
www.thehorseandhound.com

On the B4632 midway between Cheltenham and Stratford-upon-Avon, at the
heart of the village

The large village of Broadway, in the south-eastern corner of the county, is justly famous for its attractive appearance, especially the lengthy High Street with its wide, grassy verges and Cotswold stone buildings – the 'broad way' of its name leading down as the A44 (Fish Hill) from the western Cotswold escarpment. For well over a century it has been a place for sightseers to visit, from the Midlands and further afield, earning for itself the twin epithets of the 'Show Village of England' and the 'Jewel of the Cotswolds'. One of its most famous buildings, dating from 1620, is the Lygon Arms on the High Street, though this is now very much a hotel and restaurant rather than a genuine pub. One building that most certainly is, and only a little way further along the road, is the Horse & Hound.

A little younger than the Lygon Arms, and also built from warm, honey-coloured Cotswold stone, the Horse & Hound probably began life as an inn servicing the London to Worcester coaches, though by the time the village's railway station

The Horse & Hound, Broadway.

The bright and airy dining end of the pub.

opened in 1904 this trade had long since ceased, replaced by horse-drawn charabancs and, later, their motorised successors. The railway, linking Cheltenham with Stratford-upon-Avon, only lasted until 1960 but is slowly being reopened in stages as a preserved steam line under the name Gloucestershire & Warwickshire Railway, though not yet as far as Broadway.

The pub, recently refurbished to a high standard, comprises a long bar room plus a smaller dining area. Besides a range of real ales, home-cooked, locally-sourced food is on offer without compromising the pub's status as a true local. A range of pub games are available, and regular live music nights means that this pub is fully involved in all manner of community events. Accommodation is also available, for short or long stays.

The name, like many in the county, refers to the long-standing tradition of fox hunting with horses and hounds in the region.

The pub sign, with its age-old hunting name and image.

BROADWAY: CROWN & TRUMPET

Church Street, Broadway, WR12 7AE · 01386 853202 ·
www.cotswoldholidays.co.uk

Just off the B4632 midway between Cheltenham and Stratford-upon-Avon, at
the heart of the village close to the High Street

Tucked away behind the village green, close to St Michael's church and not far from the Horse & Hound, is another seventeenth-century stone inn with a heavy tiled roof. This is the Crown & Trumpet, which has featured in CAMRA's *Good Beer Guide* since 1993 and can boast, among other real ales, its own seasonal beers brewed especially for it. From the Stanway Brewery of Cheltenham, these are Morris-a-Leaping (spring), Cotteswold Gold (summer), Wizard Brew (autumn) and Lords-a-Leaping (winter). Much smaller and cosier than the Horse & Hound, it features old wooden pub furniture and log fires in its one room, with a

The Crown & Trumpet, Broadway, in 2006.

Another view of the pub, as it was when this postcard was posted on 20 August 1945. The sender's message begins: 'Enjoying my holiday immensely & having some lovely drives. I hear you had a nice V.J. Day [15 August].' *(Author's collection)*

The bar counter.

The Crown & Trumpet's sign: in comparison with the Horse & Hound, a much more unusual image.

The Crown & Trumpet's wonderful clutter of breweriana, agricultural antiques and old furniture, including that one-time pub essential now all but disappeared – a piano.

collection of brewery artefacts on the walls. Regular live music evenings are also held here, with blues and jazz a speciality, and it offers a range of traditional pub games, including one that is sadly rarely found in British pubs: ringing the bull, a game extremely simple in concept but fiendishly difficult in practice!

Traditional, seasonal dishes such as asparagus and Evesham pie (made with beef in a plum sauce), with the ingredients sourced locally, are a speciality of the pub, as are hot toddies and mulled wine in the winter. An outdoor seating area is at the front of the building – a change from the more usual practice of having it at the back – which allows customers to relax in the sunshine and watch the world and his wife pass by. Accommodation is available for those wishing to stay longer. The pub is very popular with walkers (the Cotswold Way passes close by) and other visitors intent on exploring the area.

The name Crown & Trumpet pays homage to the sovereign – the crown – and the instrument played by a herald to announce a royal visit; in this case the name can almost certainly be taken to relate to an actual visit made by a ruling monarch some time in the distant past.

CHADDESLEY CORBETT: *TALBOT INN*

The Village, Chaddesley Corbett, Kidderminster, DY10 4SA · 01562 777388 · www.talbotinn.net

Left off the A448 Kidderminster to Bromsgrove road some 3 miles out of Kidderminster

Located on the village high street opposite the church of St Cassian (a local martyr), this imposing black-and-white half-timbered building, on a stone base, is said to date back to the fourteenth century, though nothing of the original wattle-and-daub structure appears to have survived after its early sixteenth-century rebuild as two cottages. The public bar is thought to be the oldest part, said to date from 1520. The cellar, cut out of the solid bedrock, is of unknown date. There are two other main rooms, one of which – the lounge – boasts a large inglenook fireplace. Another attractive period feature is the extensive use of floor-to-ceiling oak panelling, seen to best effect in the smoke room. Outside is a large patio, pleasantly shaded

The Talbot Inn, Chaddesley Corbett.

Having a quiet chat in
the Talbot: at the bar . . .

. . . and in a cosy corner.

by a hanging vine, a beer garden and a children's play area, while upstairs is a restaurant (added in the 1960s).

The Talbot is known to have been used for brewing cider as far back as 1801, when it was kept as one establishment by the Jackson family, presumably rented from the owner, farmer John Perrins. It was bought by George Elwell's Delph Brewery in 1890, after which it was subject to the same changes of ownership as the Mug House at Bewdley (see Chapter 1).

During the late Victorian and Edwardian eras there was a marked resurgence of interest in all things medieval, real or legendary, such as Robin Hood, King Arthur, Gothic architecture and decoration, archery, Morris and Maypole dancing – in short, an attempt was made to capture the perceived spirit of 'Merrie England'. One such manifestation was the establishment of Foresters' Clubs, and the members of the Chaddesley Corbett club met at the Talbot on the Monday after the second Sunday in June in the years immediately preceding the First World War. Led by a band, they would parade around the village with their main officers dressed as Robin Hood, Friar Tuck and so on, paying courtesy calls at the more important houses in the district before sitting down to a meal at the Talbot. Later in the afternoon, games and sideshows were enjoyed in an adjacent field. The events of late 1914 put an end to such harmless jollities.

The name Talbot is not an uncommon pub name (and is sometimes seen as the Talbot Arms); indeed, there are more than a dozen pubs and hotels of that name in the county, four of which are included here. It is from the medieval talbot dog: a breed of hound, white with black spots, employed for hunting and the ancestor of the modern fox and stag hounds. The breed was named after the fifteenth-century Talbot family upon whose coat of arms it appeared. It was also adopted as a device by the sixteenth-century Earls of Warwick, adding to its popularity as an inn sign in the Midlands.

The first half of the village's name probably means 'the clearing of Ceadd (or Ceadder)' while the second half is from the family name Corbet, holders of the manor from the end of the twelfth century.

CLENT: *BELL & CROSS*

Holy Cross, Clent, DY9 9QL · 01562 730319 · www.bellandcrossclent.co.uk

Take the A491 Stourbridge Road south off the A456 Kidderminster Road at Hagley, then any of three turn-offs to Holy Cross

Situated where five country lanes meet in centre of the tiny, north Worcestershire village of Holy Cross, this eighteenth-century pub, a Grade II listed building, features in CAMRA's National Inventory of Historic Pub Interiors for the very good reason that it must be one of the least-altered pubs in the county. It seems to have been first recorded as a pub in 1810, when the landlord was Ambrose Wall, a brewer. In the dual-occupation or dual-use of those days, it was also a shop. In 1914 it was leased by the owner, William Durant Thatcher of Clent Hall, to Mitchells & Butlers, putting an end to the on-site brewing, then sold to them outright in 1932. It is now a free house once again.

By no means a large building, the Bell & Cross somehow manages to squeeze in no less than five small rooms – and corridors – complete with glazed partitions and other Victorian woodwork.

The inviting entrance hall.

The Bell & Cross, Clent.

One room is the public bar, complete with log fire, while the others – the Bottle Room, Snug, Pink Room and Old Smoke Room – are used for dining as well as drinking. All are decorated with old prints, photographs and memorabilia in the 'old pub' style so often attempted by modern designers but seldom pulled off. The overall result is an extremely well-kept, cosy village pub catering for all tastes, where long-standing regulars and first-time visitors are made to feel equally welcome.

Outside is a heated, covered patio and a beer garden with panoramic views. Named Dining Pub of the Year by the *Good Pub Guide* in 2005, the Bell & Cross is rightly famed for the quality of its food, and makes an excellent place to relax after a hard day's rambling in the nearby Clent Hills. Private parties and similar functions can also be

Barman Gary does the honours.

The Bell & Cross's intimate dining rooms.

catered for. Still with food, the Bell & Cross has one last surprise up its sleeve: chef Roger Narbett is the long-serving official chef to the England football team (he is also in charge of the Chequers pub at Cutnall Green, just south of Kidderminster – an equally-historic pub but one where the emphasis is much more on food).

The pub's name incorporates two obvious religious symbols, one being borrowed from the name of the village, the other being added in 1918.

CLIFTON-UPON-TEME: *LION INN*

1 The Village, Clifton-upon-Teme, WR6 6DH · 01886 812975 ·
www.clifton-upon-teme.co.uk/lion

On the B4204 midway between Worcester and Tenbury Wells, at the heart of the village

The little village of Clifton-upon-Teme is sited on the old saltway that once led from the ancient production centre of Droitwich to Leominster in Herefordshire, and dates from before the Norman Conquest. The name is somewhat misleading since the village is sited on the top of the ridge some 600ft above the River Teme safely out of the way of flooding; the name of the river was presumably added to the original 'cliff-farm' to distinguish it from other Cliftons. Its old manor house was built in about 1200 and was used as the village's guildhall and courthouse. Following the pattern of its time, it had one great hall with a central fireplace with outbuildings at the back surrounding a courtyard. It is thought that it also served as a hostelry of some kind from the beginning, catering for travellers journeying between Worcester and Tenbury Wells.

The Lion Inn, Clifton-upon-Teme.

The medieval chimney stack, a relic of the old manor house. The bars on the lower window on the right mark where prisoners were once confined, a reminder of the inn's past usage as a courthouse.

In 1270 the village was granted Royal Borough status by Henry III, giving it the right to hold a weekly market (every Thursday) and an annual four-day fair; both gatherings were held on the little village green opposite the manor house. Such fairs were not the funfairs they became in late Victorian times, with rides and sideshows, but rather very important trading occasions to which merchants would travel great distances to sell their wares, and to which the inhabitants of the surrounding areas would come to stock up for the year on those essential items – and non-essential luxury goods – that could not be manufactured locally.

The wonderful central hearth between the main drinking and dining areas.

Here, the ubiquitous Banks's standard lion sign, lettered to suit each specific pub, is most appropriate.

By 1600 it had become an inn under the sign of the Red Lion: one of the most popular names for English pubs, the sign's heraldic symbol has usually been taken from the arms of the local nobility, in this case the Jeffreyes family of Homme Castle (now a farmhouse) a little higher up the Teme Valley near Shelsley Beauchamp. By the late eighteenth century Homme Castle, together with the Manor of Clifton, was a property of the Winnington family, whose ancestral seat was at Stanford Court near Stanford Bridge. Changes in the family's fortunes however led to part of the Stanford Court Estate being sold off by auction in 1932, one of the lots being the Lion Hotel as it then was.

Much rebuilt (in warm red brick) and altered over the centuries, and with a number of changes of ownership since the 1932 sale, the pub has managed to retain some portions of the original manor house: the chimney stack on the outside wall is certainly medieval while the position of the fireplace in the centre of the main room is almost as old. The pub is still very much a village local – the last of three that once were here – with its darts and cribbage teams and regular quizzes and music nights. Pub meals and accommodation are also available. The Clifton Hunt has its first meeting of the season, in November, on the village green.

The Lion is reputed to be haunted by the ghost of a man aged about fifty-five, who walks about the premises.

COOKLEY: *EAGLE & SPUR*

176 Castle Road, Cookley, DY10 3TB · 01562 850184

At the junction of Austcliffe Road and Castle Road, both off the A449 Wolverhampton Road north of Kidderminster

Situated at the crossroads in the heart of the north Worcestershire village of Cookley, the Eagle & Spur was opened as a pub in 1834 by its first landlord, Joseph Morris. Until 1869 it was known as the Spin Eagle – a name of obscure origin. It would appear to have been enlarged on more than one occasion, by incorporating outbuildings and new extensions and an adjacent house. At least one other house has been demolished to make way for the pub's car park. During the nineteenth century it also incorporated a general village shop. The pub is situated only a few yards from the Staffordshire & Worcestershire Canal, above the mouth of the 65yd-long Cookley Tunnel, though it is very much a village local rather than a canalside pub, serving the workers from the numerous metal-working industries and foundries along this stretch of the canal, as well as other residents. Only one such firm remains today,

The modern, simple but eye-catching sign.

The Eagle & Spur, Cookley.

Fox's Morris, in one of their regular performances.

The turn of the women, this time the Step on Board Appalachian dancers of South Birmingham.

The light and cosy public bar.

Titan Steel Wheels Ltd – formerly Cookley Ironworks – but the staff still use the pub, so keeping the tradition alive.

Other traditions, such as regular visits from mummers and Morris dancers, are also kept alive – the Cookley-based Fox's Morris practice on Thursdays in the local school and have made the Eagle & Spur their local. (Founded in 1999, the group's name derives not from the animal but rather a pun on its origins among members of the Friends of Cookley School, or FOCS.) Yet another pub tradition, the weekly live folk music evening, is honoured every Friday; such activities have been encouraged since the pub's 2001 change of licensee.

Inside the pub are a number of rooms, all recently made over in a fairly neutral modern style, including a small, enclosed public bar or snug, a more open and spacious lounge area, a function room and a restaurant. The latter is a new venture, and specialises in home-cooked dishes made using local produce. Outside, there are tables at the front and a beer garden to the rear.

DEFFORD: *CIDER HOUSE*

Woodmancote, Defford, WR8 9BW · 01386 750234

Set back off the north side of the A4104 Pershore to Upton-upon-Severn road, west of Defford, just past the railway bridge and the Oak pub. There is no sign

As the county's only surviving cider house, this Grade II listed building is unique in Worcestershire and is one of only three in the whole of Britain selling no beer, only cider. (The other two are the Cider House at Wootten Green in Shropshire and the Olde Cider Bar at Newton in Devon.) As such it is Worcestershire's sole representative of a type of establishment once widespread in this cider-producing region but now, sadly, all but gone.

The Cider House is a small, black-and-white half-timbered building typical of the county, with a thatched roof (recently and expertly renewed). It could very easily be mistaken for a farmhouse, in both appearance and setting, that the twentieth century has thankfully passed by. What makes it doubly unique is that, despite being listed in CAMRA's National Inventory of Historic Pub Interiors, patrons sit outside the pub around the lawn at the front of the property, their drinks dispensed in timeless fashion straight from the door of a small 'cellar' at one end of the building. Here the cider is served straight from the cask, the varieties on offer including one made especially for the pub by Westons of Much Marcle near Ledbury in

The Cider House, Defford. The old bakehouse is the smaller building to the left.

Tapper the pub dog, with Oliver
Stokes at the bar: a Cider House
regular for more than sixty years.

Landlord Graham Collins, drawing cider straight from the cask
just as it always has been done.

Herefordshire. This is the deliciously
dry, 6% Woodmancote Cider. In
bad weather, there is a fall-back
position in the shape of a tiny
outbuilding that was formerly a
bakehouse, complete with its
original oven and a fierce stove. (A
former name for the pub was the
Old Bakehouse.)

The Cider House has been a pub
since at least the 1851 Census,
when it was recorded as being run
by John Hayward, a baker, and it
has been with his descendants ever
since; the current operators are

Inside the old bakehouse, a refuge in bad weather.

Graham Collins and his wife Jill. (According to the 1861 Census, Defford had eleven
pubs – or one for every sixteen inhabitants!) The Cider House is known locally as 'the
Monkey'- short for the Monkey House – though no one knows why. One explanation
is that a past landlord had a stuffed monkey on show, another is that the locals would
challenge each other to scramble over the beam in the bakehouse on which onions
were stored without disturbing them (or the nearby lampshade). The story most
favoured though is that an inebriated regular once fell into a bramble patch on his
way home from the pub and next day blamed the resulting scratches on a monkey –
the annual fair, held by the cattle-holding pens in the field across the road,
fortuitously being in residence! Like all good stories, who cares if it's true?

DROITWICH: *OLD COCK INN*

77 Friar Street, Droitwich, WR9 8EQ · 01905 774233

Near the end of a cul-de-sac, a short walk from public car parks in the centre of the town

This charming town pub – the oldest licensed premises in Droitwich – is thought to have first been licensed as an inn in 1712, near the end of the reign of Queen Anne. On the first floor it has one large and two smaller windows from the Norman church of St Nicholas, which was demolished during the previous century when the building that is now the inn was under construction. This church had stood on the corner of Friar Street and Winnetts Lane but after being commandeered as barracks by Parliamentarian forces during the Civil War, it was destroyed by a Royalist bombardment from across the valley of the River Salwarpe. (Other sections of the church's masonry survive in the walls and pavements nearby.) The whole end of Friar Street is reputed to be haunted – the Civil War and a destroyed church being a particularly potent combination – with the Old Cock Inn having its fair share of the action with a number of reports of general spookiness.

The Old Cock Inn, Droitwich.

The view from the other direction, towards the town centre, with Judge Jeffreys' head over the nearest doorway and the reused church window above the main bar room.

The principal bar room.

The town of Droitwich has flourished since at least Roman times, its prosperity built on the twin resources of salt springs for medicinal bathing, and brine extraction for salt production – a hugely valuable industry for many centuries until production ceased early in the twentieth century. Its name is thought to derive originally from the Old English for 'dirty settlement' on account of its salt pits and marshy ground, the suffix -wich in place-names becoming associated later specifically with salt-producing sites.

The Old Cock is a multi-level, wood-panelled pub that seems to tumble back down the slope from the street with a succession of small rooms on each side of a central passageway partitioned off for eating and drinking in comfort, affording its customers some degree of intimacy. It is consequently a very popular venue for meals, so much so that the Droitwich Lions hold their regular meetings there. A rather worn stone head, with a frog emerging from the mouth, over the front doorway is thought to mock the infamous Judge Jeffreys who, after the Duke of Monmouth's unsuccessful rebellion of 1685, held trials here (and elsewhere in the Midlands and the West Country) for the purpose of putting to death as many of the participants as possible. The hearings probably took place in the pub's long upstairs room.

The name Old Cock is a variant of the simpler Cock, often used to denote that the 'sport' of cock-fighting took place in the pub (or its yard); it could also mean that 'cock-ale' was sold there, this being a foul-sounding concoction of beer laced with minced meat and jelly from a cockerel.

ELDERSFIELD: *GREYHOUND*

Lime Street, Eldersfield, GL19 4NX · 01452 840381 ·
www.eldersfieldpub.co.uk

Signed north off the B4211 between Tewkesbury and the M50 Junction 2,
south of the motorway

Tucked away in the south-western corner of the county beside the Gloucestershire border, well off the main road in the tiny hamlet of Lime Street, this red-brick building dates back to at least 1873 as a pub and, until the 1960s, was known as the Butcher's Arms. Eldersfield is a very spread-out collection of such hamlets in the much larger area formerly known as Malvern Chase – a great medieval hunting forest stretching south-eastwards from the Malvern Hills to the River Severn.

The Greyhound's tiny public bar with its inglenook fireplace, stone flags and wooden panelling, is original, with the room next door having formerly been a butcher's shop at one time. The premises have been extended over

The Greyhound, Eldersfield.

the years, with two other buildings being
incorporated into the pub, and an upper storey
added; the original thatched roof was replaced
then or at a later date. The concrete path in the
front garden incorporates large, flat stones said to
be shaped in the outlines of different cuts of meat;
whether real or fanciful, the butcher connection
was certainly visibly expressed in the shape of a
large butcher's block displayed out the front,
giving rise to the pub's local nickname, 'the
Block'. It has, alas, since rotted away. The present
name was chosen by the 1960s landlord, a
member of a greyhound-owning syndicate.

The Greyhound's beer is served straight from
the barrel behind the bar in true country pub
tradition (though pubs that do so today are sadly
few and far between), and pub games are here to
be enjoyed, including the fast-disappearing game
of dobbers, also known as indoor or Evesham
quoits. Locally-sourced food is available, with wild
boar pie a speciality.

Are they cuts of meat?

Outside is a beer garden – blissfully undisturbed by traffic noise – and, accessed
via the pub, a relatively modern skittle alley housed in a second-hand military base
hut keeps another regional tradition alive. A more recent addition to the pub's
facilities is the adaption of a former barn, dated 1871, as a holiday cottage.

The Greyhound's single bar counter, complete with the
decorative swags of hops found in so many Worcestershire
pubs.

Landlord Matthew Brown drawing beer straight from the
barrel, a practice sadly now rarely found in the county.

EVESHAM: *TALBOT*

74 Port Street, Evesham, WR11 1AP · 01386 446462

On the B4035 Evesham to Banbury road on the eastern side of the Avon, about 250 yards up the hill from the Bridge Street river bridge. Limited parking

Evesham is a vibrant market town at the foot of the Cotswold Hills in the south-east corner of Worcestershire. Surrounded on three sides by a loop in the River Avon, it lies at the heart of the fruit-growing district known as the Vale of Evesham. According to the story, it was in the eighth century that a swineherd (some sources say shepherd) by the name of Eoves (some say Eof) saw a vision of the Virgin Mary beside the Avon and fetched bishop Ecgwine from Worcester to show him the exact spot. The bishop promptly decided to build a monastery there. Hence the name, from Eoves' ham or settlement. Unfortunately, the first recorded variant of the name is Ethom, in 706, from the Old English 'et' and 'hamme', meaning 'a great bend in the river' with the Eoves story probably being made up afterwards as exactly that – a good story.

Not surprisingly, given its age, Evesham is full of ancient buildings, the most famous being the ruins of the Benedictine Abbey of St Mary in the centre of the town. The only subtantial portion standing is the Bell Tower, completed in 1539 – the year

The Talbot Inn, Evesham, as it looked in about 1930, with the Swan Inn beyond. Today the scene is not much different, though the road is busy with traffic and the Swan has been modernised inside. *(Courtesy of the Talbot, photographer unknown)*

the monastery was dissolved. Also not surprisingly, Evesham was very much in the control of religious authority – but not so the then separate village of Bengeworth just across the Avon from the Abbey. This village – the name means 'the enclosure of Benna' (or Beonna) – had somewhat of a reputation for lawlessness and debauchery, no doubt engendered by the number of river boatmen who frequented its many ale houses. A few survive today, of which the oldest is the Talbot. Previously known as the Bell, it is first recorded in the 1573 parish register when, on 29 November, John Houlle of that address was buried.

The Talbot is set back a little from the main road; the paved area in front would once have been a small village green, complete with a water pump. Between 1626 and 1636 the Manor of Bengeworth was held by the Courtene family, who featured a black talbot on their coat of arms and, as the green was where the local hunt met when such things became more formalised social events, by 1758 at the latest the pub had undergone an appropriate

The pub sign, depicting the hound of its name.

change of name. (See under the Talbot at Chaddesley Corbett on page 86.)

Inside, the Talbot has an L-shaped floorplan made up of a large public bar with a long counter and two smaller, more intimate drinking areas away from the door, evidence of the fact that it has been extended over the centuries by incorporating neighbouring buildings. (The rear half of the pub is certainly older – or less rebuilt – than the grander front.) Overall, it is a warm and unpretentious local, complete with a largely Victorian decor, that has evaded modern attempts at a total makeover and, as such, is one of a fast-disappearing breed of town pubs.

Landlady Sally Keogh meeting and greeting.

The public bar.

HANLEY CASTLE: *THREE KINGS INN*

Church End, Hanley Castle, WR8 0BL · 01684 592686

Off the B4211 from Great Malvern to Upton-upon-Severn. Coming from Malvern, take the first right turn after the B4209 turn-off for Hanley Swan, just north of Upton, and continue past the school to the end of the lane

This fifteenth-century, Grade II listed pub has been described as a gem of a village pub – and it most certainly is. Though not easy to find – especially in the dark – it is well worth going out of your way to visit for it is one of the most unspoilt pubs you are ever likely to find. Seemingly cobbled together out of a brick building and a black-and-white timbered one, it has a tiny public bar (more of a snug really) dominated by a large inglenook fireplace, connected via an outside 'corridor' to a slightly larger second bar room, known as Nell's Lounge Bar, with a Victorian range in the fireplace. This room – into which live bands somehow squeeze to perform – was once part of the house next door, incorporated into the pub in the 1960s. The house latterly belonged to 'Old Nell', hence the room's name. She has been claimed to have been seen in ghostly form before the fire, dressed in her customary red bodice and skirt, black overskirt looped-up at the sides, white shawl and Welsh-style black leather hat.

There is also a family games room, with no bar, and some outside seating. Accommodation is available – ideal for anyone wishing to attend one of the pub's regular beer festivals.

The Three Kings Inn, Hanley Castle, once two entirely separate buildings.

In Nell's Lounge Bar, once part of the house next door.

In the tiny public bar.

The pub stands on the site of a medieval church house, and originally maintained that close link with the church with parish events being held in an upstairs room accessed via an outside staircase. It was also used for the all-important tithe audits. It is believed that behind the Georgian brick façade the building's timber beams, so full of character, were fashioned from fifteenth- and sixteenth-century ships' timbers – possibly readily available after the demise of the village's river traffic.

The Three Kings has remained in the care of the Roberts family for the best part of a century, and at first glance it would appear that no major refurbishment, or indeed redecoration, has been undertaken during all that time – but nor should it have been, for if it had the pub's incredible atmosphere would have been lost for certain. Any mod cons are notable for their absence. The beer is refreshingly cheap, and so is the excellent food (cooked to order), all adding to the 'time warp' experience – and anyone foolish enough to ask for lager will be deservedly laughed at. As a consequence the pub is always high on the list when awards are being handed out, and in 1993 it won the ultimate title of CAMRA's National Pub of the Year (and was runner-up five years later). It is also in CAMRA's National Inventory of Historic Pub Interiors.

The village takes its name from a long-vanished castle built by the Earls of Gloucester and Warwick, just south of the village, latterly used as a hunting lodge for Malvern Chase until demolished in the reign of Henry VIII. The village's fortunes have fluctuated over the years for it has had, at various times, its own market, pottery industry and quay on the Severn – as well as three pubs. Today it is a sleepy little backwater, bypassed by the main road, centred on the tiny green with its great cedar tree beside the fourteenth-century barn-like church. As befits its location by the church, the pub's name commemorates the Three Wise Men of the Nativity story.

HONEYBOURNE: *THATCHED TAVERN*

*12 High Street, Honeybourne, WR11 5PQ · 01386 830454 ·
www.broadway-cotswolds.co.uk/thatched tavern*

*On the corner of the High Street and China Crescent in the centre of
Honeybourne. Fifteen minutes' stroll from the railway station*

The wonderfully picturesque old part of the village of
Honeybourne lies in the Vale of Evesham at the foot
of the Cotswolds, at the meeting point of several
minor country roads. Close to the border with Warwickshire,
it is roughly equidistant from Evesham to the west
and Broadway to the south. It is also known as Cow
Honeybourne to distinguish it from its newer half, Church
Honeybourne, which lies on the other side of the
north–south Roman road now known as Buckle Street and
is a residental development built after the coming of the
railway from Worcester to Oxford. The name Honeybourne
is taken to be a reference to the sweetness of the local water
and/or grazing.

The Thatched Tavern, Honeybourne.

The public bar room and counter.

The older end of the pub, showing clearly
the supporting timber A-frame.

Cow Honeybourne possesses several fine old buildings dating back to Tudor and
Stuart times but even older than any of these is the Thatched Tavern, said to date
from the thirteenth century (though as is usual in such instances, exactly how
much, if any, of the original structure remains is open to debate). A long, wattle-and-
daub structure with tiled and thatched roof sections, the pub has a two-room bar
partially knocked-through, plus an extension at one end containing two small dining
rooms (the Cedar Restaurant) resulting from the incorporation of the neighbouring
property into the pub. Low ceiling beams and uneven, stone-flagged floors add to its
charms. The younger end of the pub underwent extensive repair at the end of 2006
when it was in danger of collapse. Outside there is a garden at the rear, with a
marquee available for hosting private functions. The pub also operates an outside
catering service, and takeaway meals are sold.

Of special interest to architectural historians is that the Thatched Tavern is one of
only a handful of surviving examples of a cruck construction, a building method in
which two whole tree trunks were pegged together in pairs to form large A-frames to
form the basic supporting structure of the building; one is clearly visible at the older
end of the pub.

INKBERROW: *OLD BULL*

The Village Green, Inkberrow, WR7 4TZ · 01386 792428

On the A422 Worcester to Alcester road, at the heart of the village

The Old Bull by the green in the charming village of Inkberrow has many claims for inclusion in this book, not least of which is that it is a perfect example of an old English village pub continuing to provide a service as an unofficial labour exchange where someone with an odd job that needs doing can find someone with the neccessary skills or equipment to do it. To many outside the village it is famous as the spiritual home of *The Archers*, since it was used by scriptwriter Godfrey Baseley as the model for the fictitious Bull public house in that long-running radio series. A small display of *Archers* memorabilia is on the walls for the benefit of the many fans who visit the pub each year. It is also said to be the most frequently painted pub in the country (by artists, that is).

The building dates back to at least the latter half of the sixteenth century and was once a farrier's shop for selling

The Old Bull, Inkberrow – alias the Bull, Ambridge.

The massive end fireplace.

In the bar.

harnesses and other items of tack. It probably incorporated, or stood beside, a smithy – the village green being the traditional and logical place for such an establishment, it having both the space and and a water pump for the waiting horses and waggons. William Shakespeare is reputed to have stayed there in 1582 on his journey to Worcester to collect his marriage licence and, if the marriage was performed in Worcester, both he and Anne Hathaway may well have stayed here on their way back to Stratford-upon-Avon. (The place of the ceremony is uncertain.) At that time the ale house was known as the Black Bull, another fairly common rural pub name. Another great frequenter of hostelries in that period – at least according to oral tradition – may well have visited it also, the person in question being Charles I, and the occasion being when he spent the night of 10 May 1645 at the nearby vicarage prior to the Battle of Naseby.

A third frequenter, though of less renown, was the local curate Edward Pearce – a man labelled a 'stirrer of strife' and who, at the local Quarter Sessions in 1602, was charged with 'riotous and lewd behaviour'.

In appearance the pub is an L-shaped black-and-white half-timbered building, one half of which is a two-storey private quarters block and the other the public area. Although nominally divided into bar and lounge, this part of the building comprises one fairly small space for both eating and drinking, complete with two fireplaces suggesting that it was indeed once two rooms. Sadly, a display of small regimental plaques that once graced one of the fireplaces has now gone. The room is open to the (windowed) roof; there are joists – where once the farrier's wares were hung – but these do nothing to detract from the wonderfully spacious feeling. The floor is of uncovered ancient flagstones, adding to the strong period atmosphere.

KIDDERMINSTER: *BOAR'S HEAD TAP HOUSE*

39 Worcester Street, Kidderminster, DY10 1EW · 01562 68776 · www.thetaphouse.co.uk

Limited parking in Worcester Street, a cul-de-sac off the one-way system inside the Ringway, so best approached on foot from one of the nearby public car parks. Ten minutes' walk from the railway and bus stations

The Boar's Head is an imposing building standing next to the now-empty indoor market. After the market closed a smaller version was held in the street outside for several months before it moved to its present, much larger outdoor site in Vicar Street.

First mentioned in a local trade directory of 1820 – the year of George IV's accession to the throne – the pub has an ornate, double-fronted brick and stone façade with a central entrance giving the customer the choice of turning right into the public bar or left into a smaller, very cosy lounge. The public bar is finished in a very basic, stripped-down style with exposed brickwork and a wooden and tiled floor,

The Boar's Head Tap House, Kidderminster. The traditional barrel pub sign, now rarely met with, indicates that here beer barrels are tapped.

The main entrance. Ornate hanging lamps outside pubs were once a common sight, their purpose being to attract and guide customers.

The public bar with its telephone kiosk in the wall.

All hands to the pumps! A busy evening in the Boar's Head.

while the lounge has upholstered bench seating and floor-to-ceiling wall panelling salvaged from a hotel in Tewkesbury and installed in 1996 when the pub was refurbished. Both rooms have iron stoves in the old fireplaces – the one in the public bar was installed when the open fire literally sparked a serious chimney fire in the 1990s. An unusual feature is a genuine (but not operational) red telephone kiosk built into the wall of the public bar. The old side entrance passageway beside the public bar was incorporated into that room during the refurbishment. Behind the two front rooms is a much larger space known as the Yard (it was formerly a courtyard) enclosed at the same time, beyond which is a small outdoor terrace.

The lounge with its reclaimed oak panelling.

Music night: local band Daddy Delux perform in the Yard.

The Boar's Head is the principal live music venue in Kidderminster, with new and established local bands and artistes performing on Thursday and Sunday nights in the Yard.

The pub's name is far older than the pub: in use since the fourteenth century, it is thought to refer to the custom of serving a boar's head, with an apple in its mouth, at Christmas. (It can also derive from a local landowner's coat of arms.) The 'Tap House' part of the name was added by Wolverhampton & Dudley Breweries to a number of its pubs towards the end of the twentieth century; strictly speaking it denotes a pub next to, or actually part of, a brewery where beer is sold as soon as it is ready for tapping.

KIDDERMINSTER: *YE OLDE SEVEN STARS*

13–14 Coventry Street, Kidderminster, DY10 2BG · 01562 822475

In the centre of the town almost opposite the Swan shopping centre and multi-storey car park

It is a useful rule of thumb that any establishment with the words 'Ye Olde' in its title is generally rather a disappointment, but there are notable exceptions to this rule and Kidderminster's Ye Olde Seven Stars is one of them. Undoubtedly the oldest surviving pub in the town, it was restored to its former glory and reopened in 2006 after a brief period of closure (and several years of neglect). In layout it comprises two rooms – the Full Bar at the front and the Back Bar behind – with magnificent wooden floors believed to have come, several years ago, from a carpet mill in the town. There is also a large patio where stables and other outbuildings once stood. The building was originally two cottages (on a plot of land mentioned in the Domesday Book), which were converted into a pub in about 1792. It has had a chequered history, being used at various times as a coaching inn, a brothel and a smugglers' den. Its closeness to the River Stour served it well in this latter regard and there are entrances to two tunnels in the cellars; the tunnels, now filled with rubble, blocked-off and unexplored as yet, were presumably employed to conceal the coming and going of contraband.

Ye Olde Seven Stars, Kidderminster – the oldest pub in the town.

Known locally as simply the Seven Stars (its original name), the pub can boast a ghost who, it is believed, frequents the cellar where she moves objects about, switches things on and off and so forth in time-honoured manner. Several people claim to have seen her in living memory, reporting a short female figure dressed in a gown and veil, all formed from a grey mist. Named the Grey Lady, she is claimed to be the ghost of either a young girl who died of natural causes in an upstairs room, or an old landlady whose mentally-impaired son died in an accident in the cellar; sadly, she still searches for him.

The new landlord concentrates on those two staple essentials of any good pub: well-kept real ales and high quality, simple food (in this case a range of filled cobs). Many other landlords would do well to follow suit, for simple is often best. A recent

The Seven Stars' front bar.

The old sign, now displayed on the terrace
at the rear.

innovation (February 2007) is that customers are encouraged to order meals from a
select list of local takeaways for eating in the pub, where cutlery, crockery and
condiments are provided.

The name Seven Stars is found all over the country and is a reference to the
number of stars in that most recognisable of northern hemisphere constellations, the
Plough. Its agricultural association made it an ideal choice for a pub name in
villages – and even towns – across the country. The constellation is properly named
Ursa Major, or the Great Bear, so pub sign painters have had a choice of images to
work from. Both the constellation and a bear were represented on Ye Olde Seven
Stars' old sign, which is now displayed at the rear of the building, while the two at
the front follows the modern trend of simply giving the name of the pub painted in a
'hand-written' style, with no illustration. (Yet another, older sign on the end wall
depicts the stars.)

MALVERN: *BREWERS ARMS*

Lower Dingle, West Malvern, WR14 4BQ · 01684 568147 ·
www.brewersarmswithaview.co.uk

Just off the B4232 West Malvern Road, opposite the turning for St Ann's Well.
Lane closed to cars – use the small car park on the main road a few yards to the
south

A small, off-the-beaten-track pub, the Brewers Arms dates back to the 1830s, when it occupied one of a pair of adjoining cottages (the second of which is now incorporated into the pub). The house was built by one Edmund Pitt, on church land – in 1837 the authorities put a stop to his using it as a public house and it was not until 1871 that it became a pub again, this time run by Henry Turle. The name Brewers Arms was first used in 1873, by the then licensee Samuel Ruck, in recognition of the fact that beer was brewed on the premises. It has long been a favourite of beer-lovers and of walkers on the Malverns and the Worcestershire Way (which runs along the road at this point), though its future hung in the balance in 1992 when it was almost destroyed by fire in the June of that year. Thankfully, it was restored sympathetically with the one room featuring tradtional-style woodwork of high craftmanship, and reopened that October. The restoration was assisted by a

The Brewers Arms, Malvern,
half-hidden down its lane.

The main entrance is on the other side from the lane, overlooking the garden.

In the bar, formerly two rooms.

The adjacent 1920s tea room, now a dining room.

fund-raising concert, in Worcester Cathedral, given by the internationally renowned violinist Nigel Kennedy, who then lived nearby. Regular music nights, though sadly now without him, are held in the pub – but no recorded music (nor television or fruit machine). Immediately outside is a small 1920s black-and-white tea room, now used as an overspill dining area (after a second life as a Sunday School).

Since a change of licensee in 2005, the Brewers Arms has become very much a community pub: on Sundays the morning papers – and breakfast – can be bought there, while on Sunday evening it is home to the Cheese Club, when customers are encouraged to bring in exotic cheeses for each other to sample, with biscuits, pickles and the like provided by the pub. The pub also sponsors two cricket teams, and two women's hockey teams, and has its own quiz team. It even publishes its own free newspaper, *The Brewers Bugle*. Home-cooked food is a speciality – and is available for takeaway.

Last, but by no means least, the pub has one more surprise up its sleeve. Walk out of the door, turn right and stroll along to the end of the raised walkway above the garden – and you will be rewarded with what, in 2005, was recognised by the trade paper the *Morning Advertiser* and the brewers Eldridge Pope as the Best Pub View in Britain. If the vista from the eastern side of the Malverns is spectacular, then the more secret one from here on the western side is doubly so, with what looks like the whole of Herefordshire stetching away towards the Welsh Hills. It has to be seen to be believed.

NEWNHAM BRIDGE: *TALBOT HOTEL*

Newnham Bridge, Tenbury Wells, WR15 8JF · 01584 781355 ·
www.thetalbothotel.co.uk

Located at the junction of the A456 Kidderminster to Leominster Road and the
A443 Worcester to Tenbury Wells road

Newnham Bridge is a hamlet some 3 miles east of Tenbury Wells, taking its name from the main road crossing of the River Rea a little way upstream from its confluence with the River Teme. The 'Newnham' portion of the name comes from the early nineteenth-century Newnham Court nearby, which in turn derives its name from the medieval Neowanham meaning 'new homestead'. (The Rea, not to be confused with the river of that name running through Birmingham, rises near Long Stanton in Shropshire and flows south for some 20 miles before joining the Teme.)

Seemingly out of place in such a setting, the Talbot Inn – yet another of that name in the county – is an imposing mid-Victorian structure built of red brick with stone trimmings on the doorways and second-storey windows, and has been described as being of railway-style architecture influenced by William Ruskin. The reason for its over-the-top, out-of-place grandeur is that it was built as a hotel for members of the Victorian upper-middle classes wanting a break from city life in the heart of the country – with a lot of fishing thrown in (as borne out by the pub's internal decoration). The railway station comparison is in fact not so far off the mark, bearing in mind that it was built a stone's throw from the earlier Newnham

The Talbot Inn, Newnham Bridge, on an undated postcard probably from the 1930s. (*Courtesy of the Talbot Hotel*)

Spot the difference: the Talbot as it is now, and
the grand entrance.

Bridge railway station, opened in 1864,
on the Great Western Railway's branch
line from Bewdley to Tenbury Wells. The
same solid architectural style was
commonly used to project an image of
substance and reliability. The railway
brought in many of the Talbot's guests –
and, every summer, visitors of a decidedly
different social class in the shape of
hundreds of hop-pickers from Birmingham
and the Black Country. Mechanisation
after the Second World War saw the
annual hop-picker invasion become a
thing of the past and, with the changing pattern of rural transport, the station
closed in 1962 – and the whole branch two years later, another casualty of the
Beeching era. From this date onwards the vast majority of the pub's customers have
had to rely on the motor car or the main road bus service to reach it. (The same
sadly holds true for so many of the county's rural pubs ever since the 1960s.)

Inside the Talbot is a traditional public bar room, a modern, more spacious lounge
and two restaurant areas. There is also accommodation available, the upstairs
bedrooms having stunning views of the surrounding countryside and the pub's own
private stretch of river. In June 2006 the Talbot was host to the first Tenbury Wells
Music & Cider Festival.

OMBERSLEY: *KING'S ARMS*

Main Road, Ombersley, Worcester, WR9 0EW · 01905 620142 ·
www.kingsarmsombersley.co.uk

On the A4133 at the southern end of the village off the A449 bypass

The village of Ombersley dates back to Saxon times and is ideally situated on good agricultural land overlooking the River Severn a little to the west. It also lies on an ancient saltway from Droitwich running straight through the village down to the river at Holt, then across and on to Herefordshire. Recorded in the Domesday Book as Ambreslege, the name almost certainly derives from 'Ambre's lege', the Old English lege meaning a clearing (for a military camp and/or settlement). It was probably also the site of a Roman camp marking a good fording place on the river.

The prosperity brought by farming, and the abundance of trees in the river valley, combined to produce a large number of half-timbered buildings in the villlage, one of which is the King's Arms. This is said to date from 1411 (and licensed from 1423) and, nearly two and a half two centuries later, is said to have provided the first night's lodging for Charles II fleeing after his defeat at the Battle of Worcester. A solid walnut bed in the pub is said to be the very one in which he slept, though it has

The King's Arms, Ombersley (the first building on the right on this postcard), dating from 1905. (*Author's collection*)

The King's Arms today, from the
car park at the rear.

been pointed out that, the bed being much shorter than the king was, he must have
spent an extremely uncomfortable night in it. The pub is named in his honour –
though not until after his restoration to the throne, as to do so before would not
have been at all wise; before then it was the King's Head.

   The pub's first recorded licensee, in 1835, was George Thompson, and it remained
a free house until 1951 when it was acquired by Mitchells & Butlers of Smethwick.
Now a free house once again, today the King's Arms is a large, sprawling, multi-
room, multi-level pub where drinkers and diners can feel equally at home: the
doorless rooms are clustered around a central bar and small enough to provide a
cosy sense of intimacy – enhanced by the pub's low ceilings and boosted
considerably in winter by its wonderful open fires. For many centuries a coaching
inn, it is an early Tudor replacement or rebuild of its medieval ale-house predecessor,
to which early seventeenth-century plaster ceilings have been added downstairs

The public bar . . .

. . . and one of
the many
secluded corners.

(complete with painted decorative mouldings). The plasterwork between the black beams of the ceilings and walls is painted white, a colour mellowed by age and smoke. Sadly, a former display of medieval armour has disappeared; happily, so have the cock-fights that were held here up to at least the 1840s. Outside there is a pleasant walled garden for use in fine weather.

ROCK: ROCK CROSS INN

Rectory Road, Rock, Bewdley, DY14 9SD · 01299 832533

Midway between the A456 Kidderminster to Tenbury Wells road and the B4202, east of Clows Top

The village of Rock is situated in one of the highest parts of Worcestershire, on a plateau some 600ft above sea level. Just south of the Wyre Forest outside Bewdley, it is close to the county's north-west border with Shropshire. Curiously, its name has nothing to do with rocks at all but is a shortened form of the early medieval name 'at ther oak' – presumably there was once a landmark oak tree here. By the thirteenth century this had become Roke, or the even shorter Rok which, three centuries later, had mutated into Rocke.

The Rock Cross Inn – another pub name with an obvious religious connotation – stands at the eastern edge of the village and is a cosy little establishment with a small public bar and two other small areas, one of which is neatly tucked away and reserved for dining – testament to the fact that the pub, like most of its kind, has had its public space enlarged at the expense of what were once private rooms. After being closed for

The Rock Cross Inn, Rock.

Looking towards the raised
dining area from one of the
bar rooms.

nearly a year, it reopened at the beginning of 2003 – very much bucking the trend
as far as rural hostelries are concerned – and has deservedly become a very popular
community pub. It changed hands again in 2006, happily with no change in its new
fortune. It was recorded as a pub in 1841 but is probably at least two hundred years
old, though detailed information is sadly lacking. It was once part of the Great
Witley Estate centred on Witley Court some 3 miles to the south of the village, one of
the most grandiose houses in the Midlands. Built in the early eighteenth century by
the 1st Lord Foley (the Foleys were a Black Country dynasty of ironmasters), it was
acquired in 1838 by the 1st Earl of Dudley who remodelled it virtually as a palace in
order to impress Queen Adelaide, widow of William IV (who had died the previous
year). In 1920 the house was sold out of the Dudley family to a Kidderminster
carpet magnate, Sir Herbert Smith. In 1937 however, it was largely destroyed by fire
and its archives – including those relating to the Rock Cross – lost.

Rock parish church is the largest Norman church in the county and a modern
variant of the traditional annual 'beating the bounds' ceremony is enacted in the
village on the Sunday before the May Bank Holiday. This fund-raising 'Pound the
Bounds' day is organised by the Rock Village Hall Committee, with a choice of routes
of different lengths to suit all ages, the longest being a 24-mile hike around the
entire parish. The walkers start and finish at the pub, which opens early in the
morning to see them off.

The height of the village, and consequently its views in all directions, make it a
favourite haunt of ramblers throughout the year, with individuals and organised
groups usually taking a circular walk from the Rock Cross. Be warned though – its
elevation above the surrounding landscape makes Rock more exposed than other
villages, leading to the expression that it is 'topcoat colder' than anywhere else in the
county – i.e. an extra layer of clothing is called for. A local story apparently has it that
when one very old inhabitant was asked for the secret of his longevity, he answered to
the effect that he thought it too cold in the churchyard to bother going there.

SHENSTONE: *PLOUGH*

Shenstone, Kidderminster, DY10 4DL · 01562 777340

From Kidderminster on the A448 Bromsgrove road, take the second exit at the Mustow Green roundabout, then immediately first right (Curslow Lane) then first right again (Back Lane) and continue into the village

This very well-hidden but very well-regarded pub is one of ten tied houses owned by Daniel Batham & Son Ltd of the Delph Brewery located at Brierley Hill just over the border in the Black Country. (Their only other tied pub in the county is the Swan Inn in neighbouring Chaddesley Corbett, which is well worth a visit.) The brewery, which supplies a number of the region's free houses into the bargain, has been in the hands of the same family since 1877 and is justly famed for the quality of its products, notably its best bitter. This is so popular that, unusually in the trade, it is supplied in 54-gallon hogsheads rather than smaller casks. (Equally good, though not always available outside the tied houses, is its dark mild.)

The sign of the Plough at Shenstone, in this instance depicting the agricultural implement rather than the star constellation.

The Plough, looking towards the modern main entrance facing the car park.

At the bar counter . . .

. . . and an ancient high-backed settle, a typical piece of pub furniture made in order to protect its occupants from draughts.

The Plough began life as a cottage, half of which became a pub in 1840, and is yet another example of an establishment that has been enlarged over the years (including here the roofing-in of the former courtyard behind the main building), resulting in a long drinking area split into the old public bar and a two-section lounge. Its present condition is a far cry from what it was half a century ago and this and its present-day popularity – it's a regular fixture in the *Good Beer Guide* – is largely down to the enthusiasm and sheer hard graft of one man, Jim Rose, a fishmonger from Chaddesley Corbett. He took over the pub in 1954 from its previous tenant, Bill Pratt, who had been in charge for thirty-five years. At that time it was very much a tiny, extremely basic, agricultural workers' pub, with beer still brewed on the premises and served from the barrel, but during Mr Rose's tenure over the next forty years a transformation took place, with expansion into the former ground-floor living area doubling the bar space at a stroke.

For fans of Led Zeppelin, the Plough will always be associated with the group: it was the local of drummer John Bonham who, before his tragically early death in 1980, spent the last three days of his life here.

Shrawley: New Inn

*New Inn Lane, Shrawley, Worcester, WR6 6TE · 01299 822701 ,
www.newinnshrawley.co.uk*

*On the corner of New Inn Lane and the B4196 Stourport-on-Severn to Holt
Heath road*

An odd-shaped building on the corner of New Inn Lane in the tiny village of Shrawley – historically part of the Vernon Estate of the Earls of Dudley – the New Inn is first recorded as licensed premises in 1832. It was run by Samuel Ford, who added the business to his existing slaughterhouse and butcher's shop in the same premises. The pub remained with the Ford family for another three-quarters of a century.

As was so often the case, the name 'New Inn' was chosen to distinguish the pub from an older inn that stood, or had stood, across the road. (Also then, just as much as today, it implied that it was 'modern' and 'up-to-date' in outlook towards its customers.)

Inside, the pub has been opened out only a little and retains two bar rooms, one of which (the lounge) now serves as a dining area. On display is an early twentieth-century photograph of the annual club day of the Shrawley Foresters, held every second Tuesday in July. After assembling at the pub they would march through the village to the church, headed by a band (usually from Stourport – see the Bird in Hand in Chapter 3). After a service, they went on to partake of refreshments at Church Farm before returning to the field behind the New Inn (now built upon) for fun and games – and presumably more refreshments of a liquid kind. (See also the Talbot in Chaddesley Corbett earlier in this chapter)

The countryside around the village, set in a hollow on the western side of the Severn, is popular with ramblers with the pub conveniently located next to the entrance to Shrawley Woods, famous for its springtime display of bluebells. Home-cooked dishes made to

The New Inn, Shrawley, with landlord Keith greeting customers at the door.

The welcoming fireplace in the public bar.

traditional old English recipes are a speciality, and full English breakfasts, sandwiches and other snacks are served all day, as well as hot drinks and cakes for anyone embarking on, or just completing, their hike. The new landlord of the pub has a refreshingly hospitable approach to walkers, to the extent that notices outside announce that muddy boots and dirty dogs are welcome. Other landlords please take note – and take up your carpets.

STANFORD BRIDGE: *BRIDGE HOTEL*

Stanford Bridge, Tenbury Wells, WR6 6RU · 01886 812771 ·
www.thebridge-stanfordbridge.co.uk

On the B4203 Great Witley to Bromyard road by the bridge over the Teme at Stanford Bridge

Stanford Bridge, a cluster of houses about 7 miles south-west of Stourport-on-Severn, takes its name from the more dispersed hamlet of Stanford-on-Teme a little to the west. This was once a village, but lost its heart – literally – when the parish church was destroyed by the Salwey family, owners of Stanford Court, to make way for a 25-acre ornamental lake.

The prosaically-named Bridge Hotel dates from the mid-nineteenth century but was rebuilt at the end of the century in the then fashionable Mock-Tudor style so

The Bridge Hotel, Stanford Bridge, now bypassed by the main road, by day and by night.

beloved of builders (and purchasers) of large, middle-class, red-brick villas. From the late-Victorian period onwards this section of the Teme Valley became increasingly popular with those seeking a respite from the industrial conurbation of Birmingham and the Black Country, with fishing on the river high on the list of genteel recreations enjoyed. As such it was a later counterpart to the Talbot at Newnham Bridge not so far away, but unlike the Talbot was never served by the railway. In the days before the motor car, its location meant that the Bridge Hotel, in keeping with its appearance, was very much a middle-class place to stay.

Bridge licensee Tim on the left: one of the county's youngest landlords.

Ironically, it was the development of the motor car at the turn of the century that led to the Bridge's principal claim to historical fame. In 1901, at the Grand Hotel in Birmingham, the Midland Automobile Club (MAC) was founded by a group of businessmen connected with the region's nascent car manufacturing industry, including Herbert Austin, J.D. Siddeley, and Fred, Frank and George Lanchester. That same year the MAC held its first hillclimb, on the Birmingham to Alcester road, but this and subsequent similar events elsewhere fell foul of the law so, on 12 August 1905 in the hamlet of Shelsley Walsh a couple of miles south of Stanford Bridge, a purpose-built 1,000yd-long hillclimb on private land was inaugurated. Regular meetings have been held ever since, making the world-famous course the oldest motorsport venue in continuous use anywhere in the world. The 140mph-plus top speeds reached today must far exceed anything imagined by its Edwardian founders!

The Bridge's connection with Shelsley Walsh is that during the early years many competitors and officials at the hillclimb meetings stayed there, though by 1930 they had decamped to the more luxurious Swan Hotel at Tenbury Wells (now converted into private residences). After the Second World War the Swan was shunned as having gone downmarket – as of course it had to in order to survive all year round – and various other hotels in the area were patronised by different individuals. By the 1960s however, the Bridge was back in favour, if only for the simple reason that it had a campsite next door, an important amenity in the more egalitarian postwar era now that motorsport was no longer a rich man's preserve. It was also attracting growing numbers of enthusiastic, but much less well-off, spectators. (A similar turn of events was taking place at the same time regarding the TT motorbike races on the Isle of Man.) Those seeking more comfort today book into neighbouring pubs and hotels, including the Manor Arms at Abberley and the Talbot at Knightwick (see Chapter 5).

The Bridge has two fairly small rooms, plus a larger separate restaurant; since a change of licensee in 2005 a whole range of events have been inaugurated, including pool, darts and quiz nights, and live music jamming on Sunday nights. In July 2006 the first Bridge Bash was held here: four days of live music, barbecues and a celebration of local cheeses and real ales, ciders and perries. For those there for the duration, the faithful campsite came into its own.

TENBURY WELLS: *KING'S HEAD*

Cross Street, Tenbury Wells, WR15 8EG · 01584 810464

On the edge of the town centre on the A4112 Tenbury to Leominster road

Although the King's Head is quite small inside, past owners and landlords of this fascinating local have so far resisted the temptation to knock through its several little rooms and corridors to make one large space. A building is recorded in the Domesday Book as standing on this site, and the current structure is one of the oldest buildings in Tenbury Wells – the 'Town in the Orchard' as it is now marketed. Exactly when it became a pub is unclear: it was purchased from Humphrey Wolverton, a weaver, in 1791 by John and Sarah Hill, who then leased it to a Philip Pound (who bought it in 1813) to run as an inn, with beer being brewed there until the mid-1920s. As is so often the case in this self-styled Royalist county, the pub's name and sign commemorate Charles II and his restoration to the throne in 1660.

The King's Head, Tenbury Wells, one of the oldest buildings in the town.

The ancient stained-glass windows.

The sign which, as is usual for pubs of this name in Worcestershire, depicts Charles II in preference to any other monarch.

Known to locals as 'the NAAFI', because of long-standing military connections, the King's Head is the regular meeting place of the local branch of the Royal Navy Associations – indeed, it is a popular town pub for a very wide range of clientele, from pensioners and other local residents to students from the nearby St Michael's College. Inside it boasts wooden and tiled floors, and old stained-glass windows. One unusual feature is the old wrought iron footrail along the front of the main bar.

There is a beer garden at the back of the main building, and a former stable block from which, in the years before the First World War, Sidney Davis & Son ran a small car hire business. A 1908 advertisement proudly boasted of 'a fine 24hp Gladiator Touring Car we have recently placed on the road for hire, in charge of an experienced London Driver. This Car will seat seven persons, is powerful, roomy, comfortable, reliable, and smart in appearance.'

Regular events, such as a weekly quiz and monthly live music gigs are held, and there are reports of a ghost – not scary but 'cuddly'.

TENBURY WELLS: *PEMBROKE HOUSE*

Cross Street, Tenbury Wells, WR15 8EQ · 01584 810301

As for the King's Head but a little further out of town

Known locally as 'the Hop Pole', this large Tudor black-and-white building has been used as a pub since at least 1600, when it was first recorded (and for much of that time as a cider house); it has been suggested that before it was built in the sixteenth century the site was occupied by a parsonage. Situated at the junction of Cross Street (the A4112 to Leominster) and the Bromyard road (the B4214), it is just on the south side of the town centre. Since the current landlord took over it has built a reputation for excellent beer and food; for the latter a small restaurant extension – the Old Piggens Dining Room – was opened in 2003 on a lower level, thus preserving a traditional, one-bar room pub atmosphere complete with roaring fire. There is also a beer garden for use in the summer.

The magnificent Pembroke House, Tenbury Wells, believed to be the town's oldest licensed premises.

Pembroke House's well-stocked bar.

The pub is thought to have been built by William Sydney, Earl of Pembroke and son of Sir Henry Sydney, Lord of the Marches and Governor of Ludlow Castle under Elizabeth I. Many original features remain, including an exposed section of ancient wattle walling. The pub was part of an endowment of Pembroke College, Oxford, and stands next to Pembroke Cottage close to Pembroke Avenue and College Court.

UPTON-UPON-SEVERN: *YE OLDE ANCHOR INN*

High Street, Upton-upon-Severn, WR8 0HQ · 01684 592146

At the river end of the High Street, opposite the junction with Church Street (the B4211)

This bustling ancient local, with its maze of small, wood-panelled rooms – complete with low beams and open fires – ranges over several different levels, all arranged around one central bar area. According to the inscription outside the building dates from 1601, though has undergone some rebuilding in the style of the original; indeed, at the time of writing a planning application has been made to enlarge the dining area at the back of the pub into the existing kitchen and create a new kitchen to the rear.

Ye Olde Anchor Inn, Upton-upon-Severn, the left-hand building on the block.

The Anchor, pre-Second World War, on a souvenir postcard. Behind it is the Star Hotel and across the road the King's Head Hotel, both establishments still very much in business as pubs. *(Author's collection)*

Blocking off the road outside the Anchor, December 2006, while work begins on the annual ritual of erecting the winter flood barrier.

As mentioned in the entry for the Swan in Chapter 1, Upton pubs cater for different groups of customers, with different interests. In the case of the Anchor, an important (and extremely popular) interest is live music, especially blues, and besides hosting regular music nights the pub is closely involved with the running of the town's annual Blues Festival.

The Anchor was very much in the vanguard of the modern micro-brewery movement in the county (see Chapter 5) with the opening, in 1983, of a brewery at the rear of the premises, trading under the name of the Jolly Roger Brewery. Two years later though, the pub changed hands and the Jolly Roger concern moved to Worcester (but has since sadly closed), the Upton brewery becoming the Old Anchor Brewery, now sadly also defunct. A less healthy episode in the pub's history – bodysnatching – occurred in 1831, as recounted in the accompanying newspaper extract below.

As is the case with Ye Olde Seven Stars in Kidderminster, Ye Olde Anchor Inn is a rare instance of the tweeness of the name outside not being reflected in the ambience inside. The 'anchor' element is self-explanatory while 'olde' is simply an old variant spelling of 'old', commonly (and erroneously) pronounced 'oldie'. Similarly, 'ye' is a variant spelling of 'the', the letter y being used in earlier times by printers to represent the Old English letter thorn; consequently 'ye' should be pronounced 'the', though almost everyone of course says 'yee'. Generally, a pub's name – in this case the Anchor Inn – would have been altered at some time to emphasise its age in order to give it an edge over its rivals.

Graves were opened at Hanley Castle churchyard and two recently interred bodies taken away. They had been sent in packing cases from the Anchor Inn, Upton-on-Severn to London, but parties following them, found them and restored them to the church. The resurrectionists were not caught.

Berrow's Worcester Journal, 21 January 1831

Worcester

A s befits its size and status as county town and cathedral city, Worcester can boast nearly a hundred pubs (plus assorted hotels and other bars), though this is perhaps only a tenth of the number that once existed. Several licensed premises in the centre date back to Tudor times and were already old when the English Civil Wars of the 1640s hit the city hard. Not all the older pubs have been treated sympathetically over the years though, but four have been selected as worthy of inclusion here (not forgetting the Anchor in Chapter 3). The city dates from pre-Roman times – the origins of the name are uncertain – as its site was an easily fortified promontory overlooking a strategic fording place on the River Severn. Consequently, it has been fought over by a long line of attackers including the Romans, Danes, Saxons and the Welsh, with the last assault occurring during the Second English Civil War. As the city grew it expanded to the north and to the south, creating one of the most impressive Georgian streetscapes in the Midlands running northwards from the Norman cathedral through the High Street, the Cross, the Foregate and the Tything. The four pubs included here are listed in the following order: north of the centre, central, then west across the river in the district of St John's.

> Yesterday a woman who lived without Sidbury Gate and goes by the name of Thirsty Martha being at the Wheatsheaf Publick House in that neighbourhood, a man offered to pay for as much Ale as she could drink while he smoked a pipe of tobacco; she accordingly drank eight pints in the Time (which was less than a quarter-of-an-hour) and went off not at all disordered, excepting that she complained that she was still dry!
>
> From *Berrow's Worcester Journal*, 28 October 1750

NORTH WORCESTER: *DRAGON INN*

51 The Tything, Worcester, WR1 1JT · 01905 25845 ·
www.thedragoninn.com

Located just north of the city centre on The Tything, the continuation of
Foregate Street, five minutes from Foregate Street station. No parking but public
car parks are within ten minutes' walk

This Grade II listed building is one of Worcester's premier pubs for real ale, and has won numerous CAMRA awards to prove it. It was constructed in about 1750 as a coaching inn, situated on the main road north out of the city, trading under the name of the George. (It was certainly listed as such in 1793.) This had been changed by 1822 to the George & Dragon, with the present name dating only from 1987.

Inside is just a single bar room, formed when the inn's two original rooms were knocked through (and the doorway into the side drive-in bricked up). Outside to the rear is a partially covered area for summer use. The Dragon is definitely not the smartest of Worcester's pubs, with the refurbishment of the 1980s now looking rather tired, though plans are in hand for a full makeover. It is however definitely a 'must visit' free house for anyone at all interested in sampling a wide variety of good

The large, single bar room.

The Dragon Inn, Worcester.

Dragon landlord Richard, behind the bar.

beers, ciders and perries of which there is a large and continually changing selection of those not often available elsewhere in the city. It is very much a true local, being slightly off the usual tourist trail (though in the middle of the string of antique shops spaced out along The Tything), but anyone wanting to experience a proper town pub as they once were, is made to feel welcome. Bar food is also served.

CENTRAL WORCESTER: *CRICKETERS*

6 Angel Street, Worcester, WR1 3QT · 01905 23583

In a short street linking Foregate with the bus station and market, 3 minutes'
walk from Foregate Street station. No parking but public car parks close by

W hat is apparently otherwise a fairly ordinary, though very comfortable, one-room, old-fashioned town pub (dating back to 1781) is included here because of its past history and its current strong sporting connection. Many pubs have such connections when located next to a football or cricket ground, but the Cricketers is unusual in that the county cricket ground to which it is linked is several hundred yards away across the river in New Road. Part of the explanation is that although there are pubs closer to the ground, none have been built next to it because of the problems with flooding there; a second reason is that at some time in the past Worcestershire players began to use the Cricketers as their preferred pub; a third is that recent licensees have encouraged them to do so, assembling in the process the stunning collection of cricketing memorabilia on display.

The Cricketers, Worcester. The Theatre Royal formerly occupied the site immediately to the left of the pub.

The central bar counter.

Worcestershire County Cricket Club was founded in 1865, at a meeting convened on 4 March that year at the Star Hotel in Foregate Street – still open but recently renamed, as part of a chain, the Worcester Whitehouse Hotel (though it retains a Star Bar). Since 1899 the club has been based at its present ground, with earlier matches played at Boughton Park further to the west beyond the city.

The Cricketers did not begin life as a sporting pub though – far from it. Before 1992 it was variously the Shakespeare Tavern or Shakespeare Hotel, erected when a travelling theatre manager, James Whitley, built the Worcester Theatre (opened 1781), together with the Shakespeare next door, in Angel Street. An early licensee – if not the first – was a Mr R. Hurdman, listed as being there in 1793. In 1805 the theatre was renamed the Worcester Theatre Royal. In 1877 it burnt down and was rebuilt, then refurbished in 1902 as the New Theatre Royal and Opera House. As

Part of the impressive display of cricketing memorabilia.

with many regional playhouses, it fell victim to changing fashions in entertainment and in 1955 was forced to close. Five years later it was demolished and replaced by a car showroom (later a mini-supermarket) of unsurpassed ugliness. Throughout all that time though the Shakespeare maintained its close connection with the theatre – it even had direct access from it to the pit and stalls, while the theatre's green room, where the company relaxed, was upstairs. After the theatre closed the link naturally faded away with only the name hinting at what once was. Then, in 1992 the pub took on its present name, and a whole new identity, currently reinforced by the fact that the landlady's husband, Adrian Dowling, was formerly the cellarman at the cricket ground. It was refurbished in October 2006, with a new sign replacing the old weathered one (which featured a portrait of the most famous English cricketer of them all, W.G. Grace).

Home-cooked food is available at the Cricketers at lunchtime, and the drinks on offer include real cider and a large choice of malt whiskies. Bed and breakfast accommodation is also available, as well as a private function room. The pub can also boast two ghosts – a male and a female – who move things about, but are said to be friendly.

CENTRAL WORCESTER: *PLOUGH*

23 Fish Street, Worcester, WR1 2HN · 01905 21381

Just off the cathedral end of the pedestrianised High Street, a short walk from Foregate Street railway station and the bus station. Use one of the numerous city centre car parks

Running between the High Street and Deansway (the A44), the short thoroughfare known as Fish Street possesses several timber-framed buildings dating back to Tudor times. Tacked on to the end of these, on the corner with Deansway, is the Plough, a comparative stripling dating back to at least 1822 as a pub. (The Deansway is a modern relief road bypassing the pedestrianised High Street; it chopped-off half of Fish Street and necessitated the remodelling of the end of the Plough.) It has a rather unprepossessing appearance at present, owing to a combination of its location on a busy main road, its corner entrance and the bland rendering on its walls. Inside however is another matter entirely. After a long period of neglect the pub closed in August 2005 but happily reopened in new hands in the spring of 2006, cleaned and rejuvenated as befitting its Grade II listed status after the city planners refused a change of use application to turn the premises into solicitors' offices.

The Plough in Worcester, at the end of the truncated Fish Street, with its unusual side entrance.

The Plough's internal layout could be described as somewhat unusual, and dictated by its corner site and the slope of the ground on which it stands: a narrow entrance hall has steps up to a small bar counter, off which is a small room on each side. (The bar continues on into one of these.) Outside is an equally small patio area, walled-off from the main road. The woodwork is painted a light pastel green, matching the original paintwork found after the later layers were stripped away. Combined with the several windows, this results in a very airy and surprisingly spacious feel to the rooms.

The back of the Plough. Note the wall sheltering the rear terrace, and the remodelled end of the pub.

One of the two similar bar rooms.

Alan Grainger, Chairman of CAMRA's
Worcester Branch, raises a glass to the
award-winning Plough.

Upstairs is a private function room – once a darts and pool room until it was
realised that the floor could not safely take the weight! Good quality food is served,
ranging from simple bar snacks to full meals, and a range of some half-dozen (often
locally-produced) beers and ciders.

The Plough was the Worcester branch of CAMRA's Pub of the Year for 2006.

WEST WORCESTER: *BELL INN*

35 St John's, Worcester, WR2 5AG · 01905 424570

From Worcester city centre, cross the river and follow New Road past the cricket ground, take the second exit at the roundabout and then second left into St John's. There is no parking – use the small public car park at the end of the road

T he western district of Worcester immediately beyond the river bridge is known as St John's, and was formerly St John-in-Bedwardine, a township in its own right before it was incorporated into the city from 1837 onwards. As such, it had its own ample supply of public houses, several of which remain in business. (Somewhat confusingly, one of the district's principal thoroughfares is also named St John's, and it is on this busy street that the Bell Inn is located.) The old name is thought to derive from 'Beda's wordign', or enclosure, to which the name of the dedicatee of the fourteenth-century parish church (originally chapel) was later added.

As a medieval township, St John's had several rights and privileges, one of which was the holding of a fair (more of a market in modern terms) on the Friday before Palm Sunday.

The Bell's distinctive sign, advertising Mitchells & Butler's beers.

The Bell Inn, Worcester, viewed from the churchyard opposite.

The connection between the Bell and St John's fair was that the building on the site of the Bell, known as Church House, was where a Pie Powder Court was held, its function being to run the fair, collect tolls and so forth, and also settle complaints against or between traders. (The strange name is in fact a corruption of the French *pieds poudreux* or 'dusty feet', deriving from the notion that the court had to dispense justice before it had time to shake the dust off their feet.) The court was originally presided over by the Prior of Worcester, replaced in 1461 by the Bailiff (Mayor) of the city, and last sat in 1814 when the fair ceased; the name was revived early in the twentieth century for an annual gentlemen's social evening held until about 1914, though the outbreak of hostilities that autumn finally put paid to it. When the occasion warranted it, the building's cellars were used as cells – and are now said to be haunted by a ghost who clinks the bottles and glasses down there.

The Bell's single, three-sided bar counter, remodelled in the 1950s to project out, where the old dividing wall had been, into the enlarged public bar.

The entrance corridor, looking towards the skittle alley. Note the most unusual (for a pub) sliding door to the bar on the left, immediately beyond which is a serving hatch for discreet 'outdoor' purchases.

   Church House was sold in 1816 to raise money for repairs to the parish church; at that time it comprised four small dwellings for impoverished church widows. It was then believed to have been remodelled as the Bell Inn, for the name was certainly recorded just four years later.

   Behind the Bell's plain but pleasing late-Georgian façade is a small but busy pub where the emphasis is on good (especially locally-brewed) beer, comprising a public bar – once two small rooms knocked through in the 1950s – and two smaller snugs, all simply furnished in an unostentatious manner; behind these is a skittle alley and a courtyard, accessed from a side alley, for parking bicycles. In coaching days the pub was a posting inn, where horses could be changed, for journeys on to places further west such as Great Malvern, Hereford or Leominster.

   With the coming of the railways the Bell settled down to a less frantic life as a community pub, though another mode of transport entirely was to play an important part in the pub's history from the latter quarter of the nineteenth century onwards. Although a very crude bicycle of a sort, worked by cranks, had been invented by Kirkpatrick Macmillan of Dumfries in 1839, it was not until 1873 that the first chain-driven prototype appeared. Twelve years later the Rover Safety model went into mass-

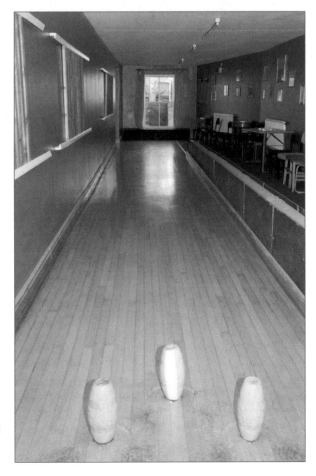

The skittle alley at the rear of the pub. (This ancient game is also known as nine-pin bowls, the direct ancestor of modern ten-pin bowling).

production, incorporating virtually all the features of the bicycle as we know it today, and a new craze was born. Cycle clubs sprang up all over the country: a perfect outlet for the young (and not so young) of both sexes to meet and mix freely, all in the name of healthy exercise, touring the countryside on roads untainted by the internal combustion engine. One such was the St John's Cycle Club, founded in 1888 and still going strong today as one of the oldest cycle clubs in the country (though it did not admit women until 1944), which still meets regularly at the Bell.

Ten Commandments

1.   When you **Lie** – Let it be with a pretty lady.
2.   When you **Steal** – Steal away from bad company.
3.   When you **Sleep** – Sleep by yourself.
4.   When you **Swear** – Swear by your country.
5.   When you **Drink** – Drink at . . .

**THE MUG HOUSE
CLAINES, WORCESTER**

6.   A man is kept in the yard to do all the cursing and swearing at this establishment.
7.   A dog is kept to do the barking.
8.   Our chucker-out has won 99 prizes, and is an excellent shot with a revolver.
9.   The undertaker calls daily for orders.
10.   In God we trust, all others cash.

From the Claines Mug House leaflet, op. cit.

FIVE

Brew Pubs

> My Beer is good, my measure just,
> Forgive me please, I cannot trust,
> I have trusted many to my sorrow,
> So pay to-day and owe tomorrow.
>
> From the Claines Mug House leaflet op. cit.

There was a time when almost every pub or ale-house brewed its own beer, the practice originating with medieval alewives brewing small quantities in their backyard for sale to friends and passers-by (as well as for their own household needs). By the time the Industrial Revolution was well under way, the late eighteenth century economies of scale had begun to take effect, with more and more villages having one or more breweries supplying other inns. (A small town would support several such producers.) The overall number of breweries was still very large though, as deliveries were confined to an area that could be served by a horse and cart – the famous brewer's dray – in a day. Then, with the establishment of a national rail network, a succession of mergers and takeovers led to the creation of regional and even national brewing centres such as Birmingham and the Black Country, Burton-upon-Trent and London. The brew pub was doomed.

By the time CAMRA was founded in 1971, there were just four brew pubs left in the whole of Britain, in rural or semi-rural backwaters. Interestingly, of these four, two were over the border in Shropshire and one – the Old Swan (familiarly known as 'Ma Pardoe's') – was in Netherton near Dudley, once part of Worcestershire but now in the West Midlands. Today there are more than a hundred – though many more have come and gone over the years – of which a total of four currently are to be found in Worcestershire. Behind this astonishing resurgence lies a combination of factors: brewery workers, made redundant by the relentless acquisition and closure policy of the big brewers, who wished to continue in their chosen profession; home-brew enthusiasts' decision to turn their hobby into a livelihood; the availability of relatively cheap and reliable micro-brewing plants – plus many thousands of real ale lovers more than willing to seek out and support the new establishments and their products.

The needs of the new generation of brew pubs are much the same as those of the old: a converted outbuilding, a micro-brewery plant and a skilled brewer; only the technology (and regulations) have changed. This is the immaculate Brandy Cask Brewery, Pershore, behind the pub of the same name.

Worcestershire's four brew pubs are of this modern generation, in terms of the brewery, though the pubs all have an earlier history of their own, with a new chapter very much in the making. They are described here in alphabetical order of place.

> And malt does more than Milton can
> To justify God's ways to man.
> Ale, man, ale's the stuff to drink
> For fellows whom it hurts to think.
>> A.E. Housman, *A Shropshire Lad*

> Turkey, heresy, hops and beer,
> Came to England all in one year.
>> One of many variants of a sixteenth-century rhyme

Strictly speaking, beer is ale (made from malted barley) brewed with the addition of hops to impart bitterness. A Dutch innovation imported during the fifteenth century, this style of brewing soon displaced the old, the words 'ale' and 'beer' later becoming synonymous.

KNIGHTWICK: *TALBOT HOTEL*

*Knightwick, WR6 5PH · 01886 821235 · www.the-talbot.co.uk ·
www.temevalleybrewery.co.uk*

*At the first junction on the B4197 north off the A44 Worcester to Leominster
road at Knightsford Bridge*

The Talbot at Knightwick, run for more than two decades by sisters Annie and Wiz Clift, is one of three pubs in Worcestershire with a national, rather than just a regional, reputation. The Old Bull at Inkberrow is famed for its *Archers* connection, the Fleece at Bretferton is known for its history and National Trust status, while the Talbot is famous for the quality of its food and drink and the emphasis it places on the local sourcing of produce and ingredients – and has a fistful of awards to prove it. As such it appears regularly in newspapers, magazines and food guides, and on radio and television, as an establishment at the vanguard of what has become known as the 'slow food' movement, of which that self-same local emphasis is such an important part.

The Talbot Hotel, Knightwick in 2007.

Knightwick, Talbot Hotel.

The Talbot Hotel as it appeared on a postcard probably dating from before the First World War. *(Author's collection)*

The pub is located close to the Herefordshire border by an old, now bypassed, bridge over the Teme, in that river's tranquil valley. The Teme rises in mid-Wales, and flows through Ludlow in Shropshire and Tenbury Wells in Worcestershire before joining the Severn below Worcester. The river has never been navigable for boats of any size; indeed, it is said – and has been demonstrated – that its bed can be walked from source to mouth, hence its valley has not suffered greatly from industrialisation. Believed to date from the late fourteenth century, the Talbot was formerly a coaching inn, ideally situated where the road from Stourport-on-Severn joined the road between Worcester and Leominster. In much the same way as the Talbot at Newnham Bridge and the Bridge at Stanford Bridge (see Chapter 4), it derived a good part of its income during the late nineteenth and early twentieth centuries from well-heeled visitors enjoying a few days in the country, usually with fishing as the principal leisure activity. As with its namesake at Newnham Bridge, the Talbot was helped greatly in this by having its own railway station nearby, this being on the Great Western Railway's branch from Worcester to Leominster, which utilised the Teme Valley for much of its route. Opened in 1874, the station closed in 1964 along with the surviving, eastern half of the line. The name Knightwick means 'the dairy farm of the knights or warriors', indicative of the agricultural nature of the region.

Inside, the Talbot has a single, cosy lounge bar with a good number of real ales always on offer, including its own brews; this in turn leads to equally welcoming dining areas. In the latter, a range of seasonal and local dishes are served, using home-grown organic salads and vegetables, home-made pies, preserves and black pudding, home-baked breads, locally gathered wild foodstuffs and locally sourced meats, cheeses and the like. For obvious reasons, some fish is not local but delivered from Wales and Cornwall. Furthermore, suppliers are named so that customers can be reassured that the ingredients are indeed as local as possible and have not had to be transported the length of the country.

Accommodation is also on offer, with day tickets for fishing close by on the Teme available. The principal catch is chubb, roach, barbel and perch, with the occasional pike.

The bar counter, the beer pumps dispensing the pub's own Teme Valley brews.

The bar, with its strangely-shaped stove almost filling the great fireplace opposite the counter.

Outside, in keeping with long-standing county traditions, Morris dancers perform here, and mummers' plays are staged. Plough Monday is the first Monday after Twelfth Night and the Victorians instituted a special church service for the preceeding Sunday, naming the day Plough Sunday. At the service ploughs and other agricultural implements would be blessed to ensure a good year for the farmers, and the practice was revived at the Talbot in 2005 with an open-air service held during the appropriate Farmers' Market (one is held on the second Sunday of every month on the stretch of old road outside the front of the pub).

The pub's micro-brewery, known as the Teme Valley Brewery, was opened in 1997, and supplies the Talbot along with a handful of other pubs and specialist off-licences. It prides itself on using only English malts and Worcestershire hops to produce a wide range of year-round, speciality and seasonal cask ales and bottle-conditioned beers. Every year in the autumn the Green Hop Beer Festival is held to

Inside the Teme Valley Brewery
behind the Talbot, with Head
Brewer Chris Gooch . . .

. . . hard at work.

One of the brewery's seasonal beers, the 4.1% The Hop Nouvelle, brewed using green First Gold hops at the time of their annual local harvest.

mark the hop harvest, a feature of which are the beers brewed using green hops – that is, those used straight from the fields without being dried to lose their moisture, as is otherwise the normal practice to prevent them rotting. The brewery's mainstay, more conventional beers (of various strengths) are named This, That and T'other. Capacity has been increased since the brewery's early days and now stands at some fifteen barrels a week, one barrel being a brewing measure of 36 gallons.

PERSHORE: *BRANDY CASK*

25 Bridge Street, Pershore, WR10 1AJ · 01386 552602

On the B4084 between the end of the High Street and Pershore Bridge
over the Avon

S ituated on the south-eastern edge of the attractive Georgian town centre of Pershore, the Brandy Cask backs onto the locks and weir complex on the River Avon just upstream of the medieval stone road bridge spanning the river. It overlooks the low-lying flood plain to the east. The bridge – superseded by a concrete one in 1926 – was rebuilt by the monks of the Benedictine Pershore Abbey after an abbot and his retinue were drowned when their boat capsized while they were crossing the river. (It was also blown up by Royalist troops in 1644 during the Civil War – drowning forty of them in the process.) The name of the town is believed to derive from the Old English for 'osier bank', reflecting its riverside situation.

The Brandy Cask, as a building, dates back to Tudor times, when it was used as a warehouse for holding wool brought in from the surrounding district for taking down river to Bristol before being exported. Towards the end of the eighteenth century (the exact date is uncertain) it became the Liquor Vaults, owned by Henry J. Baker,

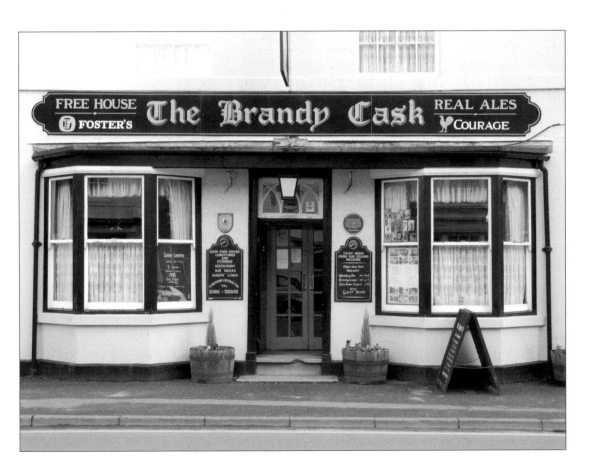

The Brandy Cask, Pershore.

Licensee and brewer Spencer Cooper keeps a watchful eye on things.

the change of use presumably brought about by a downturn in the wool trade. Here beer, wine and spirits were stored for sale to the public, dispensed either in bottles or straight into a jug. About this time the building was given a new façade, and it remained with the Baker family until the First World War, gaining the nickname 'Baker's'. It is thought that customers could also sample the wares on offer, an arrangement formalised shortly before 1921 when, as a pub, it was bought by the Hunt Edmonds Brewery of Banbury and renamed the Brandy Cask, an allusion to its former role. The first landlord was a retired policeman by the name of Septimus Octavius Collett – the seventh son of an eighth child. Later owned by Mitchells & Butlers, it was bought back into private ownership in 1990 by licensee Spencer Cooper.

In layout, the Brandy Cask is a conventional, busy town pub of its type, with one bar serving an L-shaped drinking area; there is also a restaurant to the rear. Outside, a large beer garden slopes down to the river, making for an ideal vantage point from which to watch the lock in action.

The Brandy Cask's principal, but tragic, claim to fame is that on 29 May 1943 it was hit by Wellington bomber X3704 doing a flypast during a Second World War 'Wings for Victory' week in the town. The plane was supposed to do a shallow dive towards RAF Pershore at Throckmorton, a little to the north-east of Pershore, when it somehow lost a wing and one engine on its approach, hit the tops of the buildings on the west side of Bridge Street, then took the roof off the Brandy Cask on the east side of the street. It finally crashed into the back gardens by the river. Fragments of the aircraft, and live ammunition, were found in the pub's garden for several years after. The five personnel on board – pilot G.S. Hynam DFC of the Royal Canadian Air Force, wireless operator P.E. Zoeller of the Royal Air Force and three ground crew along for a joyride, Corporal Allen and Aircraftsmen Bande and Garvell – were all killed. Hynam and Zoeller are both buried in the Second World War section of Pershore cemetery; the only other person injured – slightly – was Mrs Berry, the landlord's wife. A framed account of the whole sad story, taken from the local newspaper, is displayed on the wall of the pub.

Spencer Cooper in the brewhouse. . .

. . . and relaxing beside the Avon at the bottom of the beer garden.

The Brandy Cask is home to the small Brandy Cask Brewery, formally opened on 1 June 1995, which began brewing that May in the old bottle store (formerly a meat store) behind the pub; its three regular beers (in order of increasing strength) are Whistling Joe, Brandy Snapper and John Baker's Original. The name of another strong beer, Ale Mary, is a punning reference to the town's major tourist attraction, the early fourteenth-century Pershore Abbey. The brewery also produces a plum ale each year for the August Farmers' Market and Plum Fayre – the surrounding area being famed for its growing of Pershore Emblem, Pershore Purple and Pershore Yellow Egg varieties of plums. The last of these is the oldest, having been found growing wild in 1827 in a nearby wood.

UPHAMPTON: *FRUITERER'S ARMS*

Uphampton Lane, Uphampton, Ombersley, WR9 0JW · 01905 620305

Coming north from Ombersley, take the first left after the A4133 joins the A449

Located down a short but narrow lane midway between the main Worcester to Kidderminster road and the pretty little hamlet of Uphampton, the Fruiterer's Arms has long been a 'must-visit' for the county's real ale lovers.

The original cottage at the heart of the pub dates back to before 1848 for in that year it was bought by Thomas May, a seller of fruit, who promptly turned one of its rooms into a bar, selling beer brewed on the premises. The brewing ceased during the 1930s but the pub remains in the hands of the May family – an unbroken period of licence transfer that is said to be a record for Worcestershire, though the Cider House at Defford (see Chapter 4) certainly challenges it. The building has been

The Fruiterer's Arms, Uphampton, looking back down Uphampton Lane towards the A449.

The old public bar . . .

. . . and the more modern lounge, deliberately styled to remain in keeping with the age of the pub.

extended over the years and now comprises a plainly furnished public bar and a more homely lounge, both rooms served from a connecting bar; this layout thus preserves the traditional 'upper' and 'lower' class distinction between the two main rooms that was very much a feature of old pubs but which has now largely been swept away in favour of one-room bars.

Brewing on the premises recommenced in 1993 in a converted cider house behind the pub, the enterprise (which is separate from the pub) being entitled the Cannon Royall Brewery. It currently produces five regular milds and bitters which, in ascending order of strength, are named: Fruiterer's Mild, King's Shilling, Arrowhead Bitter, Muzzle Loader and Arrowhead Extra. Seasonal and other special beers are also brewed. With production limited to some sixteen barrels a week, sales are primarily to local outlets though the brewery achieved national recognition when, on 1 February 2006, it began supplying real ale to the House of Commons.

Three of the Cannon Royall Brewery's beers, available in bottles as well as in casks.

The village name is first recorded in the thirteenth century as Uphampton (with variants Ophampton and Huphamton), meaning 'the settlement [Old English hamtun] on high ground'; other -hamptons in the immediate neighbourhood, running northwards, include Northampton, Sytchampton, Dunhampton and Comhampton.

WEATHEROAK HILL: *COACH & HORSES INN*

Weatheroak Hill, Alvechurch, B48 7EA · 01564 823386

West off the A435 Alcester road south of the Wythall roundabout into Hill Lane, then continue on into Weatheroak Hill

Weatheroak Hill is a small dormitory village in the north-east corner of the county, about 3 miles to the south of Birmingham and roughly equidistant from the A441 to the west, the A435 to the east and the M42 to the south (the nearest access point is Junction 3). It also lies on the former Roman thoroughfare of Icknield Street, here reduced in status to a mere country lane. The origin of the name is obscure: recorded as both Wederoke and Wederokes Hill in 1299, it could equally well derive from the Old English words for weather or sheep, or from a person named Weder or Wedera, plus the suffix -oak.

In the public bar, the oldest part of the pub.

The Coach & Horses Inn, Weatheroak Hill, is an ideal place to have a quiet Sunday lunchtime meal or drink.

Enjoying a pleasant drink in good company in the garden of the Coach & Horses.

The old hamlet gives its name to the road on which the Coach & Horses stands. This is a long, narrow, white-painted pub dating back to 1780, that has been extended several times up the hill to form a multi-room, multi-level building. It has different areas, furnished in different styles, set aside for drinking or dining. The oldest part is the small, cosy bar complete with open fire and original quarry tiles on the floor. The result is a pub where the dedicated real ale enthusiast and the good food lover can both feel at home, with a reliable local clientele strengthened by visitors from further afield. At the front, on the quiet road, is a large beer garden which is very popular on sunny days.

The Coach & Horses had a rather gruesome brush with serious crime when, in March 1885, an inquest was held there into the death of Police Constable Jim Davies, from the nearby village of Beoley, who had been found stabbed to death in a field on the morning of 28 February that year. His murderer, a known thief, poacher and hen-stealer by the name of Moses Shrimpton, was apprehended in Birmingham four days later, tried at Worcester Assizes on 6 May and found guilty. Executed on 25 May, Shrimpton was the last man to be hanged at Worcester gaol; the final macabre twist in the story was that the hangman did not take into consideration the weakened physique of the 65-year-old murderer and the drop almost tore his head from his shoulders.

On a far lighter note, of special interest to the real ale enthusiast is that this free house is home to the Weatheroak Brewery. It hosts regular beer festivals, and has won numerous CAMRA awards. The brewery was established in 1997 in one of the pub's outbuildings, by agreement with the pub's owners. It began commercial production the following year and expanded in 2000. At the time of writing it has a capacity of twelve barrels a week with four regular brews – all bitters. In rising order of strength these are Light Oak, Weatheroak Ale, Redwood and Keystone Hops. Seasonal ales are also produced to suit the occasion.

NOTICE. — Will the Lady or Gentleman who stole two glasses on Sunday, kindly hand their names over the counter when they will be presented with four more to make up the half-dozen.

From the Claines Mug House leaflet op. cit.

ACKNOWLEDGEMENTS

We would like to thank all those licensees and their staff whose friendliness, patience, and unfailing willingness to answer questions helped make the research of this book such a pleasure; we are especially grateful to them for giving us permission to photograph so freely, and to reproduce examples of their own material. We also wish to express our appreciation to the many pub regulars who happily made time to speak to us – passionately – about their local's history. Special thanks must also go to Margaret and Karen for their uncomplaining forebearance during our long days and nights of absence while diligently researching this book.

Published sources consulted include county and local histories, various CAMRA publications (including back issues of *What's Brewing* and the *Good Beer Guide*, and national and regional pub guides), local newspapers and magazines, trade and street directories, general town and county guides, and sundry histories of pubs and brewing.

The purr-fect place to spend a spring afternoon: the Brewers Arms, West Malvern.